Where to Now?

T0339774

Where to Now?

Short Stories from Zimbabwe

edited by
Jane Morris

'amaBooks

ISBN 978-0-7974-4648-9
EAN 9780797446489

Published by 'amaBooks
P.O. Box AC1066, Ascot, Bulawayo
amabooksbyo@gmail.com
www.amabooksbyo.com

To be published in the United Kingdom in 2012 by Parthian
www.parthianbooks.co.uk

Cover Design: Veena Bhana
based on a photograph of a sculpture by Arlington Muzondo
arlingtonmuzondo@yahoo.com

'amaBooks would like to express their thanks to the Beit Trust, the
Association of Little Presses and Alliance Française de Bulawayo for
making this publication possible.

Snapshots, by NoViolet Bulawayo, was previously published in New Writing from
Africa, Johnson & King James, 2009.

Contents

A Beast and a Jete	Mapfumo Clement Chihota	1
Christina the Colourful	Barbara Mhangami-Ruwende	7
I am an African, am I?	Mzana Mthimkhulu	21
Making a Woman	Thabisani Ndlovu	29
Snapshots	NoViolet Bulawayo	42
Her Skin is a Map	Raisedon Baya	56
Crossroads	Novuyo Rosa Tshuma	63
The Piano Tuner	Bryony Rheam	74
The Poetry Slammer	Nyevero Muza	80
Alone	Fungai Rufaro Machirori	90
They are Coming	Christopher Mlalazi	102
Mr Pothole	Diana Charsley	109
The Accidental Hero	Murenga Joseph Chikowero	115
Sudden Death	Blessing Musariri	124
Tomato Stakes	John Eppel	133
The Need	Sandisile Tshuma	140
Glossary		147
Contributors		149

A Beast and a Jete

Mapfumo Clement Chihota

Bulelwa is a woman of amazing stamina, particularly when angry. Single-handed, she carried everything of hers out of my room: the clothes, the blankets, the washing machine, the double bed, the kid.... Nompi, her cousin, had run out of the gate and disappeared as soon as she saw that things were getting out of hand. Chikoko, my friend, had picked up one of *my* blankets, wrapped himself up in it and gone to doze on an easy chair in the lounge. I had watched her take her stuff out before banging the front door shut, and retreating to my messed up room, to sleep on the floor.

"So, have you ever witnessed a divorce or a separation taking place?" I ask Chikoko, just to start a conversation that might massage our hangovers a bit. We are in the kitchen preparing 'lupper', an ambiguous meal taken some time between lunch and supper. This set Chikoko off.

"I was a kid when I witnessed one and, up to now, I am not sure I really understand what happened." Chikoko pauses to toss a whole tomato into the lupper, then continues. "You see I had this uncle who imposed strict rules on everything in his household. But the one rule that made him almost kill, if it was broken, was that no one should ever, *ever*, set foot in his little *piri piri* garden. The garden was planted close to the wall of his bedroom-hut, and he tended it personally. It was extremely beautiful. Imagine four or five short rows of *piri piri* plants with pods at various stages of ripening: some deep-green, some yellow, some orange, some red.

"Two things happened to create a myth about Uncle's *piri piri*. His wife gave birth to a second set of twin sons. And he almost killed the first set for straying into the *piri piri* garden, after their plastic ball had fallen among

1

the plants. The myth was that uncle's testicular strength must surely come from the *piri piri*. Why else should he almost kill to protect the plants? And how come he sired sons in sets, when other men strained to produce daughters who came one at a time? Soon, every man in the village desperately wanted to eat Uncle's *piri piri*. Some even began to befriend my usually taciturn uncle in the hope that he might, one day, share the *piri piri* with them. My uncle would watch these 'strategic friendships' grow, then wait. When the issue of the *piri piri* was finally broached, Uncle would react in a non-verbal, but very disturbing way. First, he would laugh to himself, striking his palms against each other and shaking his head in disbelief, like a man shocked by a neighbour's request to share his wife. Then, quite abruptly, he would start frowning. Uncle's frown was famous. It started from the mouth then slowly climbed up to the forehead, which it furrowed so deeply that the overall efect was that of a piece of cow dung drying in the sun. Most objects of this severe frowning would just turn tail and run. The more audacious ones would stammer a few apologies then quickly change the subject, never to raise it again.

"But all this only made the villagers more curious and keener to taste Uncle's *piri piri*. One man came in the middle of the night, and it is said he failed to see or feel a single pod on any of the plants. For his efforts, he got such a bad knock from Uncle's *knobkerrie* that he ended up with a permanent lump at the back of his head – another 'exhibit' proving the worth of the *piri piri*. By now, the *piri piri* had attained legendary status. Its value began to be calculated in terms of how many chickens one might trade for a single pod. These calculations got to my aunt's ears. Being some kind of an entrepreneur, she realised that these were perfect conditions for business. Secretly, Aunt started peddling Uncle's *piri piri* in small, highly-valued quantities, but, only when she was sure Uncle had travelled far from the village. The business, however, only lasted one week. Uncle knew each pod on each of the plants by size, shape and colour. He could also tell the difference between the way he plucked off a pod and the way anyone else might. I happened to be there when he confronted my aunt about the missing *piri piris*. He simply stammered something like, 'Who, who, who, ta, ta, touched, ma, ma, my, pi, pi, pi….' Aunt did not wait for him to finish. She just got up and started to run. She was wearing a red dress. Uncle was wearing green and yellow overalls. We watched the green-yellow chasing the red till both colours disappeared behind a hillock on the horizon. That was the last time I ever saw my aunt. I was due to return to boarding school the next day and all I know is that when I returned to the village, four months later, Uncle had a different wife. Just like that!"

We sigh, as usually happens at the end of a story. "So, your uncle was already married again, four months later?" I ask.

"He was, and he was to marry someone else before my second-term holidays ended," Chikoko says, then explains, "My uncle's second wife was a very religious woman. She belonged to the Mai Chaza sect, you know, those people who wear long, white robes all the time? Yaah. Now, this woman lived with two of her nieces – young girls just entering puberty – who used to laugh a lot and frolic all over the yard. Then there was a terrible fight between Uncle and his second wife. Can you guess what happened? My second aunt caught the bigger one of the girls tending Uncle's garden. And Uncle just standing there and doing nothing about it! So she demanded to know what else the girl was allowed to do, which *she herself* wasn't. And for how long her intimate friendship with Uncle had been going on. The fight degenerated into a suicide attempt. Uncle had to catch his wife when she jumped off a tree branch with a noose around her neck. That was when he gave her a severe hiding. We could see white cloth flying about as they struggled. When they returned to the yard, one was swollen, and the other, taciturn. My aunt just packed her bags and left with *one* of the nieces. The other one remained to become Uncle's wife, up to now."

"Your uncle must be a real beast," I comment, stirring the lupper.

"Yaah. And such beasts are lucky. Because they rarely meet *jetes*."

"What is a *jete*?" I ask, out of my depth. Chikoko laughs, rubbing his palms briskly as he usually does when assuming the role of instructor.

"A woman who kicks her husband's bum around. Not necessarily the shrew or the termagant. But the dominant type. The type who defeats her husband mentally and outwits him at every turn...."

I am reminded of my own aunt, Vanyemba, who had to be tried at the headman's court when her husband caught her lying under the village builder in the middle of a maize field. The story goes like this. Her husband saw them lying down in that space between two rows of maize. When he saw them from a distance he couldn't contain himself, so he screamed and started running towards them. My aunt and her lover disentangled, and then ran in opposite directions. My uncle's fundamental mistake was that he ran after the builder, rather than after my aunt. That was a mistake for two reasons. First, the builder outran him. After chasing him for almost a mile, he gave up then hurried home to deal with his wife. He realised the second reason why he had made a mistake the moment he stormed into his wife's kitchen-hut. There she was, sitting serenely in the middle of a large group of women who were all chatting and laughing loudly. She was dishing out a meal of *sadza* and vegetables.

"Good evening Madyira," she called out cheerily, pausing to smile brightly at him.

"You say good evening, good evening to me when you have been sleeping with Mujubheki in the maize field?" There were gasps and susurrations all around. The *jete* in my aunt instantly took over. She reacted like someone witnessing the beginnings of a madness which must surely portend doom for the entire village.

"My grandmother sleeping in the anthill!" she exclaimed, holding her head as if to prevent it from exploding. "Come and witness this bad omen for me! What? Madyira! What? Me? Sleeping? With whom? Where? When? And in what manner?"

The matter ended up at the village headman's. My aunt brought eight witnesses who all testified that they had been sitting with her in her hut while Madyira was seeing whatever visions he was seeing in the fields. The women testified that they had stopped by my aunt's homestead on their way back from the Thursday Afternoon Women's Club. They had been with my aunt as she cooked *sadza* and vegetables on her kitchen fire. They even said that Vanyemba appeared like someone who had not been to the fields at all that day. They had not seen any mud or soil on her hands or legs. Her legs had even shone with Vaseline, from what they could remember. At this point, Madyira burst out, accusing all the women of complicity in adultery. This drew grumbles from their husbands who were also sitting in the crowd. Madyira was scolded for jumping into the testimony before his turn. "When children clamour for the soup ladle, the quietest child always wins it," observed *Mudhara* Ndori, who had been listening to everything and staring deeply at Mujubheki, who sat apart from everyone else, staring – in turn – at his big cracked feet. "Let us hear what Mujubheki has to say." Mujubheki refused to speak, claiming that his chest was 'too full'. After pronouncing his inability to speak, he started twitching his big ears, which grew at right angles to his head. That was the point at which Kadyevhu, the village comedian, decided to interfere with the proceedings. Directing his attention at Madyira, he asked, "You say you found the builder on top of your wife?"

"Yes."

"And you say he ran so fast that you couldn't catch up with him?"

"Yes."

"To me, that would suggest only one thing. The builder had not yet 'delivered' when you interrupted him. Because a man who has 'delivered' cannot outrun one who has been keeping his stock." Everyone laughed. Even Mujubheki's full chest lightened long enough for him to release one hyena-like guffaw.

It was now time for the headman to deliver his verdict. All the *vadare*, those gathered, listened attentively as he spoke. "This case is clearly in the open, like the driver of a tractor," he began, in his thin quavering voice. "Madyira's wife was at home cooking for her neighbours while Madyira was busy chasing some animals that he mistook for people, in the bush. The truth is like a head with horns. It cannot be concealed in thin coverings. But in this case, what Madyira claims to be the truth is so hidden than no one else can see it. What makes it so difficult to believe Madyira is that he did all the wrong things. First, he chased the wrong animal, which outran him, as we have all heard. But I want to point out, here, that even if Madyira had managed to catch this animal, his case against Vanyemba would still not have been proved. The animal might simply have told him that it had been mounting *another* animal, and not the woman accused here. So the animal's crime would simply have been that it used Madyira's maize field as a bedroom-hut, without Madyira's permission. Anyhow, when he got home, after chasing the wrong animal, Madyira found that his wife had already cooked *sadza*. *Sadza* takes time to cook, unless it is a half-cooked *mbodza*. Instead of accepting the plate that his wife offered him, Madyira refused to eat, so he himself does not know if that *sadza* was a *mbodza* or not. Everyone else who ate says the sadza was well-cooked, which means Madyira's wife could not have been the same person who had just run off from the fields. All of Madyira's suspicions are therefore impossible to prove. Our elders used to say, hit the dog on the spot where you find it shitting. For once the dog leaves that spot, it no longer understands why it is being punished. From the way I see this case, Madyira is like a man who wakes up one morning then begins to accuse his dog of a crime which it committed during its puppyhood. This court does not entertain such cheek. Instead, it deals harshly with men who bring such stale, unproven cases before it."

In the end, it was Madyira who was asked to pay a fine of three goats. One would be given to Mujubheki, whom he had falsely accused; one to his good wife, whose innocence had been proven in front of all the *vadare*; and one to the *dare* itself, which meant that the goat would go into the headman's personal flock. Vanyemba, the *jete*, had won. It is rumoured that she was already pregnant when this case was tried. Eight months later, she gave birth to a baby boy whom they called Mazheve, because he had big ears growing at right angles to his head.

We both laugh, rather weakly, when I finish telling Chikoko this story, then start to eat. The lupper is a disaster. The *sadza,* which Chikoko cooked, is clearly a *mbodza*. The stew, which both of us cooked, has too much *piri piri* (which I added). Chikoko coughs on that, and then asks if I entertain certain myths about *piri piri*. Before I can answer, my phone rings. It is Bulelwa, wanting to know why I always tell her to get out of my life each time we quarrel. She sounds wounded, although she is the one I caught kissing another man in a dark corner of the nightclub. I laugh at a sudden thought. Either she is a *jete*. Or I am a beast. Or, ours is a rare combination of beast and *jete*.

Christina the Colourful

Barbara Mhangami-Ruwende

The rickety old bus sends up a plume of red dust and black smoke pours from its exhaust pipe as it trundles up the gnarly hill towards the acacia tree with its umbrella shaped foliage. A motley group of children run behind the bus, through the billowing cloud of dust and smoke, shouting "Masvingo *netara!*"

On a boulder sit two women both dressed in long red skirts, white cotton shirts and white head scarves. I wonder, for a fleeting moment, how they manage to keep their shirts so white in Chivi where water is the colour of weak tea and the home made soap is mustard brown. Maybe God keeps their shirts whiter than white because they are good, God fearing women, fervent in their godly works.

"*Mhoro*, Kuda. How are you, my daughter?"

One of the holy women, Mai Farai, is directly in front of me. I gaze into her kind brown eyes and try to respond. My tongue will not move, but I desperately try to greet her with my eyes.

"Kuda, speak when grown-ups talk to you! This behaviour of yours is very rude." Mai Farai seems very upset with me. I try very hard to say something but the look on her face makes it even more difficult.

"Leave her, Mai Farai," shouts her friend. "I don't know why you are bothering yourself with that girl. That is how she is – a sullen child with no respect for her elders."

Mai Farai walks away, but not before casting a dirty look my way. I am used to looks like that. I let my eyes wander.

On any other day I would stand behind the acacia and watch people as they wait for the bus with the resigned patience of *kumusha*. The bus has no timetable and one is never sure whether it will hiss and heave up the hill

7

towards the acacia on any given day. My Uncle Mhike says it all depends on whether there are enough passengers to warrant a drive all the way *muchakasara moma* Chivi. I have to explain why I like to watch people waiting for the bus. I imagine what their destination might be. I give each of them a destination that I have only heard of: Harare, Chinhoyi, Beitbridge, Chirumhanzu and Mount Selinda, the ultimate destination. Only passengers who smile at me get to go to Mount Selinda. Mount Selinda is the reason I am at the bus stop today.

Two nights ago I overheard my mother telling her co-wife, my father's second wife, that my Aunt Christina the Colourful had been summoned home by her brothers – my father and his siblings.

"*Vanababa* have called her home and I think this time she will be thoroughly dealt with. It's about time too. They have let her carry on with her disgraceful behaviour for far too long." My mother smirked, tightening the *doek* on her head.

"I know what you mean," replied Mai Kuziva. "I feel so embarrassed when I hear other women at the stream talk about her and the shame she has brought on this family. It's terrible."

My mother and her co-wife make me sick. They hate each other's guts and yet at the news that someone has been summoned to a *dare,* they suddenly become the best of friends. They both take perverse pleasure at other people's plight. Last time it was the goat herder who came home with three goats missing from the herd. After a thorough whipping with strips of leather that left his back crisscrossed with angry red welts like a road map, he confessed that he had sold them in order to pay for his mother's hospital bill. I felt so sorry for him, but my mother and her co-wife had stood in the doorway of the kitchen like two cowardly thieves, delighting in his screaming and his begging for mercy. This time it was my Aunt Christina over whose fate they were gloating. Witches!

I have a feeling she will arrive on the bus that has gradually made it up the hill with one final, definitive roar and a puff of black diesel fumes. The bus comes to a violent halt, which throws the passengers forward and then back onto their seats with a thud. I have been on the bus a few times to Masvingo with my mother and, believe me, it is not a pleasant experience. The ninety minute ride from the acacia before the dirt road meets the tarred road is horrific. The bumps on the road have everyone bouncing up and down in their seats as though on a trotting donkey. The dust swirls through the holes in the floor, the roof and the sides of the bus, as well as the windows, which rarely close. Sometimes there are no windows to close, just gaping holes. The dust leaves a grainy feeling in nostrils and eyes, and passengers are loathe to bring their teeth together in case they crunch fine grains of sand. The heat, dust and smell of diesel and unwashed armpits leave me nauseous and suffocating. I snap out of my reverie as I remember that I have to warn Vatete Christina of the impending meeting to interrogate her about her wayward life.

The conductor kicks the metal door open as the bus hisses to a stop. The door creaks open and hangs precariously on one hinge – the top one. It flaps back and forth like a broken wing on a pigeon. "St. Mary's – Kurazi-Maringire – Mandiva, Masvingo *netara!*" bellows the conductor, adjusting the cap on his head and stepping off the bus to ticket the on-coming passengers. The bus boys climb as agile as monkeys onto the luggage-laden roof to unload suitcases and strangely shaped packages wrapped in brown paper or thick plastic. A goat bleats piteously from the roof. Passengers call out descriptions: "The blue one." "The brown suitcase." "The yellow bag."

The disembarking passengers are worn out. They look as though their insides have been given a good shake and that they are about to throw up the fermented contents of their sour stomachs. All except one passenger, who suddenly appears in the doorway. She surveys her surroundings from the bottom step with disdain. Her nostrils flare slightly as she looks over the heads of the passengers at the shabby view before her. There is nothing to see but emaciated children, dust and isolated clumps of dry grass. I peer expectantly from behind the acacia and I notice how the conductor's voice softens and becomes playful as my aunt lightly steps off the bus. "*Saka rini, when?*" he asks. He pointedly looks at her breasts and licks his lips like the perpetually hungry mongrel dogs littered all over the village.

"Give me two days," replies my aunt, smiling so that her cheeks are dimpled.

The waiting passengers shuffle their impatience and the conductor barks at them: "*Mari! Mari! Mari!* Bring out your money."

I watch her. She is a tall, slender woman with dark skin the colour of mulberries. Her shaven head sits gracefully on a long elegant neck. She has these charcoal black eyes which spit fire when she is angry and sparkle like sunlight on a bubbling brook when she is happy. My Vatete Christina is stunningly beautiful, the most beautiful woman I have ever seen. Not that I have seen that many. I have walked through the village with her, sometimes to Berejena Mission, and everywhere we go, people stare. The men really like her and are friendly. Sometimes too friendly. One man fell over his feet outside the bottle store and a crowd of people who were watching him gawking at my aunt roared with laughter: "Ha ha ha. Look at how he tripped over his loaf of bread feet, all because of a pretty woman."

The women cannot stand her. They suck their teeth as she walks by and none of them greet her the way the men do.

Once, a woman started beating her husband up, on the way from the miller, when he stopped to stare at my aunt as we walked by. His donkey shook the sack of mealie-meal off its back and bolted while the fat woman pelted her skinny husband with her fists. "Foolish man! Imbecile! You will catch that donkey today or I will kill you with my bare hands. What? All because of that whore?"

Even as he got the beating of his life, the man still managed to mutter "*Sis Kiri. Muribho?* Are you well?" My aunt threw her head back and laughed long and hard. I joined her, much to the woman's fury.

"Ehe, you whore! Going about stealing other women's men. You have no shame. *Hure!* God knows why you ever come back to this village bringing your cursed body with you."

My aunt marched up to the woman and stood in front of her, silently commanding her to stand up from her seat on top of her husband. The woman's chest was heaving and I saw a faint flicker of fear in her eyes as my aunt towered over her fat, wobbly body.

"If your dog bites," she said with a cool, menacing calm, "put a muzzle on him and tie him to a tree. If you fed him well, he would not be so viciously hungry now, would he?"

My aunt drew herself up to her full height, dwarfing her stout adversary even more. "If you ever in your miserable, fat-choked life, call me *hure* again, I will show you that thing which makes me and you both *hures*. I get paid, and what do you get? A grey, aging donkey, sick looking baboons you call children and this thing you call a husband?" She gazed over the woman's lumpy body and sweat drenched face with her fiery black eyes. With that, she turned abruptly and grabbed my hand. "Kuda, let's go."

I pull myself back to the present and I see her approaching the acacia. She has seen my head protruding from behind the tree trunk. "Kudakwangu!" she yells in her raspy voice. Vatete always sounds like she's been crying or screaming. Her voice has a gravelly quality that men seem to like. She decided many years ago to change my name from Kudakwashe, which means God's will, to Kudakwangu, my will. You see, I am one of six girls, the last born. There is a big gap between girl number five and me. The year I was born she was writing her 'O' levels. All my other sisters had left home and were married in different parts of the country. My father's cattle kraal was once bursting with livestock, thanks to hefty *roora* paid by my sisters' husbands. My sisters never visit. When my grandfather died, they sent word that they would come after the funeral, but none of them ever showed up to throw a stone on their own grandfather's grave.

"Ehe! It is as it should be," my mother said to her co-wife in that all knowing voice of hers. "A married woman should stay put in her husband's home or else she will return to find her place taken over by a mongoose." This is what she calls husband thieves. Mongoose are known for invading chicken coops and stealing eggs.

"*Ah ah maiguru*. Whether you keep watch over a man by day and sleep with one eye open at night, when he decides to eat from another woman's pot, you can never stop him. Those girls should come home to see their parents. It is the proper thing to do."

My mother sucked her teeth and stormed off to the back of the kitchen hut. She called out in an authoritative voice, "*Mainini*, your stew is burning over here, quick quick!" The co-wife must be reminded of her place as a junior wife, otherwise she might grow wings.

The story is that my mother, in an effort to prevent my father from taking a second wife, fell pregnant with me, sure that she would have a male child. Her mother had convinced her that God in His infinite wisdom and mercy had saved the best for last and would grant her male issue, to rid her of the shame of an all-girl household. They had even visited a *nyanga*, a wizened old medicine man who lived in the mountains, who had cleansed her womb and assured her that it would henceforth only carry male babies.

It is with this assurance that my father ran to the clinic on the day I was born to see his only begotten son, the last born. The white doctor at the clinic had told both him and my mother that this was to be her last pregnancy, otherwise she might have a child who would be mentally slow, run through the village naked, and try to bite chunks out of passersby. My father met an auxiliary nurse who congratulated him on the safe delivery of a bouncing baby girl. My aunt says my dad deflated like a tyre with a loose valve and muttered, *"Aiwa. Kudakwashe.* It is God's will."

That is how I was named, out of a fatalistic resignation to the will of God. I was not my father's will, and I was certainly not my mother's. But I became my aunt's will, her desire. I am because she is.

My aunt says not everything is the will of God, but that people are mostly responsible for the terrible things that happen. She hates the way people attribute events to God.

"Someone is stabbed in a beer hall brawl, it is God's will, someone dies at the clinic because there is no doctor, it becomes God's will. The government hikes up food prices and does not hike up people's salaries, God has decreed this too. No wonder this country is decaying quicker than a bloody carcass on a hot day!"

I hug Vatete Christina and I reach over to take her bag from her. *"Aiwa* Kuku *wangu!* It is way too heavy for you, *mwanangu!* How are you my child? Did you miss me?"

I nod my head vigorously and smile shyly at her, making sure not to bare my teeth, which I am told are too big for my mouth.

"Smile for me, Kuku." I smile, a small smile at first, then a big smile, making my aunt laugh.

Vatete rubs my head and we start walking towards the homestead. I notice how the dusty children who were chasing the bus have vanished as suddenly as they had appeared at the back of the bus.

I have to warn my aunt about what awaits her at home. I stop and I will the words to leave my head, to go to my mouth and animate my tongue. Nothing....

My aunt and I are very different. She is one of six children and is also the last born. But all her siblings are boys. She is loud and fearless, ready to fight any man or woman any day or night. Quick to anger, she says and does whatever she likes. Her brothers do not scare her the way they scare all the other women of the family. My father is the eldest and therefore the head of the family, but she calls him a toothless bulldog to his face. She was not even scared of her own father, who was hard hearted and cruel.

She wears tight jeans and miniskirts. She paints her lips red; "as though she has eaten a piece of uncooked liver," my mother says with a disgusted smirk on her face. But I know my mother is jealous. All the women secretly envy her even while they gossip about her. She paints the rim of her eyelids with a black pencil and puts a dot just next to her mouth, on the left

12

side. Sometimes she wears a wig with hair the colour of dry grass in winter. It is long and hangs down her back. Her shoes have high spiky heels and, when she walks, she sways her round buttocks left then right in a rolling motion so she does not topple over. They look like two children playing under a blanket. The buttocks, I mean.

Once I heard my uncles saying that *mahure* paint their faces and wear short skirts to entice men with their bare thighs. They were sitting under a syringa tree drinking *masese* and occasionally grabbing their crotches, sniffing the air for aromas of food wafting from behind the kitchen hut. None of my uncles is married, so my mother and her co-wife cook for them.

My aunt says that the Impulse she sprays over her body is her signature scent. "When I walk by they will know that Christina the Colourful is on her way here, has been here or is here, somewhere, somewhere." Then she throws her head back and laughs long and loud.

I am the opposite of my Aunt Christina. I am short and have a lighter skin tone, almost orange. I am stocky, round and very quiet. I don't really know if I am quiet because I have heard it said that I am quiet, or whether I am quiet because I have nothing to say. I heard my mother tell her friends at the stream that I only learnt to say a few words when I was four years old. She told them that I am slow and had to repeat grade 3. At thirteen I am only in grade 5. "That very night that I got home from the clinic after giving birth to her," she said loudly, hands on her hips, "the man announced that he had decided to marry a second wife to give him as many sons as I had given him all these liabilities to feed and fatten for another man's household. I cried and begged and pleaded. I even said I was ready to get pregnant as soon as was possible but he wouldn't hear of it. He shouted, 'No more cockroaches! That is all that can survive in your womb. All those cows I sent to your people and nothing to show for it but parasites.'"

My mother continued, milking the moment for all it was worth. "My own mother even told me that I had a stubborn womb that refused to take in a male child and that my husband could not be blamed at all for taking another wife. After all he had given me six good chances."

Her friends all piped in with their false sympathy. Inside I knew they were gleeful and happy that it was my mother who had suffered this shame, not them. "Sorry my friend, sorry *vaSawhira*. Men can be so wicked. Is a girl not a human being? Is it not girls who are taking care of their parents, sending money from the city to help out? The liabilities are those brothers of his who are a total waste of space and air," exploded one friend.

13

"Anyway," my mother clapped her hands together dramatically, "it was God's will that he take another wife because I fell ill after that and she took care of Kuda here." She pointed in my general direction. My mother never looks at me, even when she is talking to me. "She fed her porridge with cow's milk because my breasts dried up. Not a drop of milk."

"*Hee*! How can such an awful thing happen? *Yowee, yowee kani*!"

They all clucked and clapped their hands, reminding me of the chickens who aimlessly roam our yard pecking at the ground and clucking hysterically at nothing in particular.

"Yes. That woman, my co-wife, is a godsend, and we are so happy together."

I cannot believe my mother could lie so effortlessly. She is totally believable and yet I know how much she hates her co- wife. She hates the fact that my father no longer looks her way. He no longer eats her food while looking at her as if she was the food itself. He no longer visits her hut at night and I no longer hear the whimpering, groans and sighs that used to bounce off the walls of her hut. They thought I was sleeping. He has eyes only for her co-wife, who, on most mornings, saunters across the yard humming, her legs and hips moving as smoothly as the chain on a well oiled bicycle. "Look at her! Walking like she has a gold mine between her thighs," mutters my mother on such mornings.

I am the cause of her predicament. I am the reason why her co-wife has the gall to kiss her husband openly and laugh with wild abandon, slapping hands with him and making a mockery of her misfortune. I am the reason why she was pretending to these village gossips that she was happy and fulfilled co-habiting with her co-wife and their husband.

"*Heee,* but here is the funny thing: my co-wife has had two girls back to back." My mother looked at her rapt audience for the effect of her pronouncement.

"Yes, that's true, that's true," they all chorused.

"She has refused to fall pregnant again and she told my husband that two women having all girls for him means that he is the one to blame. She told him that we are only giving him what he has put inside us. She says she will not risk another pregnancy because of this foolish man, who shoots only females and then blames the women for carrying them. Must we swallow them?"

"She has a point," said one friend, head to the side, a hand on her chin.

"*He he he,*" my mother laughed without humour. "She even told him to take another wife, she does not care. She wants to be left in peace to raise her daughters."

"I am sure she got beaten to within an inch of her life." said Mai Tambu, the big hefty one, urging my mother on.

"A beating from whom? Rather you should be asking whether she beat him up. That woman is crazy. My husband would never dare to ever raise his voice at her. Useless man. He won't beat her because he is addicted to her honey and without it he will fall sick and die."

"*He he he!*" they all guffawed, like a chorus of hyenas at the sight of an abandoned carcass. I stood quietly by, watching them slapping each other's palms. I wonder what is so funny about honey and wonder where she keeps her bees.

"Vatete," I start. My tongue is loosening in my mouth, "They are waiting for you."

"Oh, them. I know, my child. Don't worry. Bunch of idiots! I am ready for them. Let us get home first then you can watch your aunt perform. You can write about the show in your book. Are you still writing?"

"Yes Vatete, I am still writing," I respond.

I inhale the musk fragrance coming off my aunt's body in waves and feel what must be joy and comfort. It bubbles from the pit of my tummy all the way up to my head, like the orange fizziness shooting its way out of a thoroughly shaken bottle of Fanta. I listen as she chats vivaciously about her life in Mount Selinda. I want to ask her when she moved from Mutare, but the words remain stuck in my head and refuse to move to my mouth where my tongue lies lifeless and heavy as a baby's wet nappy.

My Aunt Christina has an amazing way with words. When she describes something it comes to life right in front of your eyes. She uses plain words to create stories, the way a basket weaver skillfully uses long blades of grass to weave intricate patterns on his baskets. She has given me an exercise book and after she finishes telling me her stories, I write them down. She does not visit often, but each time she comes home, she reads my stories. They are all about her. She brings all sorts of tales when she comes home and I live from visit to visit in anticipation.

"Mount Selinda is a beautiful place, Kuku. It is a quiet little town that sits high up on a hill. The air is fresh and the trees and grass are lush and green, not like this back of beyond, desert wasteland called Chivi." She spits the word Chivi, curling her top lip as though she is uttering a curse, then she spits on the ground for good measure.

"I work at a bottle store there and I have a room at the back. The owner is kind and generous. Kuku, kindness is such a rare thing, you just take it when it is given to you no matter who it is from or what the cost might be."

Suddenly she looks sad and my heart breaks. My aunt should have no room for sadness in her colourful life and I am a little frightened to see it. As I am scrambling for words to cheer her up, she suddenly looks up and continues brightly, "In the morning, the air is crisp and smells of fresh grass and pine trees. It is very cool so people are not sweating and smelly the whole time. You'd think that with the scarcity of water here, people's bodies would hold on to all the water they can. Instead their bodies just expel the water in buckets of sweat."

She pauses briefly, and then continues. "I have lots of friends there Kuku. Even the bottle store owner is my friend. His name is VaMpofu, but he says I should call him Lisbon. He doesn't charge me rent and he pays me extra when his wife is away in the village. Then there is my friend Tongai who drives a *Gonyet*. He drives from Zimbabwe to Mozambique, or to Zambia and on to the Congo. His truck is so comfortable and I sometimes drive with him from Mt. Selinda to Beitbridge on his way to South Africa. I wait in Beitbridge for a few days just hanging out with friends and then he picks me up on his way back. My other good friend is a white farmer, Mr Todd. Can you believe he speaks fluent Shona, Kuku? He likes it when I call him *Mandebvu* because he has a thick bushy grey beard. He gives me lots of money and he even gave me some gold jewellery that he said his wife would never miss. He says she is cold and mean and she doesn't understand that he has an African soul, even though he is a *murungu*. His wife is very angry with him because he refuses to leave the country like other whites are doing. She wants to go over the seas, but he says his home is here."

My father's compound is in view now and my aunt straightens her back, squares her shoulders and holds her head high. She is marching towards the homestead and I have to trot to keep up with her.

"*Ah*! Vatete Kiri *vauya*!" yells my mother in her perfect fake-happy voice. She runs towards us, one slipper falling off her foot. She stops to slip her foot back into it as her wrap unravels at the waist. She stops again to secure it. She is such a good liar. She embraces my aunt as she would a long awaited friend and grabs her bag from her hand, all the while shouting "Aunt Kiri is here."

My father emerges from under the syringa and comes slowly towards my aunt. I can feel the fire in her as she gets ready to do battle. She glares at her brother, chewing hard on her bubble gum and he shocks us all by patting her on the back and shaking her hand, tugging so hard that it looks as though he is trying to pull her arm off at the shoulder.

The rest of the day is calm, with a suppressed tension hovering over the entire compound. Even the goats and the chickens seem subdued. My aunt seems unaware of the furtive glances that everyone throws her way. My uncles look cleaner than usual, wearing their best shirts. Village women are busy cooking in big black pots on cooking fires scattered across the back yard. Some of them slaughter chickens by the chicken coop. I sense that something is afoot. I do not think all this preparation is simply because of my aunt's visit. I wander around the compound, trying to guess at what could be going on.

At dusk, smells of food infuse the still air and I see a line of people snaking their way up the road towards our compound. I stand by the wooden gate and watch the multi-coloured snake inching closer and closer. The sun is now a deep orange, and it sinks to the horizon where it breaks apart like an egg yolk, spilling forth orange, red and yellow and painting the wisps of white clouds.

"*Mhoro*, Kuda." I am shocked out of my reverie by greetings from people at the gate, but my tongue remains stuck to the roof of my mouth. Some carry packages while others balance calabashes of drink on their heads. There must be at least fifteen people.

"This sullen child. Honestly, if she was mine, I would beat some manners into that vacant space in her head."

I look down at my grubby feet to avoid the scorn and accusation on their faces as they stroll past me. I decide to go and find my aunt and tell her of this latest development. I am sure Vatete Kiri will be able to explain to me what is going on. I meet my mother carrying a tray with a huge mound of *sadza* on it.

"Kuda, go and help the women carry the food to the guests under the trees. They are waiting, hurry up."

I wander towards the group of busy women and my eyes search for my aunt. She is not among the women with cloths wound round their waists with the President's face jiggling on their ample buttocks as they move about with energy and purpose. No one notices me, so I decide to go and hide behind the syringas, where I have a clear view. I recognize all the faces. There

17

are calabashes of *mahewu* and Chibuku where the men are seated on chairs and stools. The women are all seated on grass mats and goat hides on the ground, talking in muted tones amongst themselves. I realize that most of the people are from VaNyaka's compound.

"Mai Kuziva, bring Christina out now." Everyone is suddenly quiet as my mother's co-wife escorts Vatete Christina to the gathering. My aunt looks surprised to see the gathering of people. Mai Kuziva looks like a brown ant next to my aunt, who looks like a butterfly as she gracefully strides forward. Vatete looks questioningly at Mai Kuziva, who flashes her a reassuring smile and quickly averts her eyes. Mai Kuziva walks at a meek pace, her head slightly bowed and I sense that she is willing my aunt to do likewise. But Vatete continues boldly, her stride unbroken and her ample buttocks rolling. I watch as my aunt gets to the gathering and sits down on the goat hide reserved for her and Mai Kuziva, right next to my father.

My father begins: "Christina, my sister. We summoned you home two weeks ago, and we are glad that you have come."

He clears his throat. "You see, there comes a time in a woman's life when she must settle down and have her children before time runs out. Women are not like men, whose time never runs out, except in death. A woman is like a flower, whose blooms fade and die after a short time. So too do a woman's beauty and fruitfulness. They come to an end."

There are murmurs of approval from the gathering and lots of nodding heads. My aunt scans the visitors, as though looking for someone in particular. My father drones on: "Your life, jumping from town to town, is very unbecoming of a woman from a respectable family such as ours."

My aunt's eyes have narrowed like a mean cat. Her mouth twitches faintly at the corners, her bosom is heaving.

"Therefore Kiri, my only sister, we, the male members of the family, have taken it upon ourselves to find you a husband. We have done this in consultation with our ancestors, who have spoken that our father is not resting peacefully. His soul will be at peace once you are a married and dignified woman in her husband's house."

Delighting in his own oratory, my father continues with passion: "We have found a suitable husband for you, my sister. He is a mature man who is much respected in this community and will be able to take care of you and your children when they come. He has agreed to marry you despite your character flaws and the fact that you are no longer a *mhandara*. He is willing to overlook that you have been with many men, but he expects total fidelity to him once you are married."

From the corner of my eye I see VaNyaka and another man walking slowly towards the clearing. They stand by the huts directly behind my father, waiting for a cue from him.

"VaNyaka is a great farmer and I trust that you, Kiri, will be a good wife to him and you will live peacefully with your two co-wives."

VaNyaka moves to stand next to my father and I immediately feel a wave of pity for him. I take in his well-worn black trousers, tied at the waist with a makeshift belt woven out of sisal. I look at his crusty feet encased in rough *manyathela* sandals made out of strips of old car tyres. His grey shirt has a *chigamba* patch of red fabric neatly sewn on to the sleeve to cover a tear. He is grinning, showing off his brown tobacco stained teeth, which look like loose kernels of roasted maize. His beady, bloodshot eyes find my aunt. His grin widens.

For a minute I stop breathing because I do not want to miss anything. Vatete stands up and draws herself to her full height. She is wearing a black T-shirt, a calf length red skirt and *pata-patas* on her feet. There is murmuring from the visitors because it is disrespectful for her to stand up in the presence of men without being told. But my aunt does not care about such 'useless protocol' as she calls it.

"My brothers, thank you very much for this occasion and for caring so much about my welfare that you found me a husband." She reaches into her bra and pulls out a roll of money. "However, it is very unfortunate that VaNyaka here has come too late for my hand in marriage. I hereby pay my own *roora* and marry myself. Since I am damaged goods, second hand material, this money should be enough."

Vatete tosses some notes at my father and, in the ensuing commotion, she marches off to our sleeping hut without a backward glance. There is confusion and anger on the faces of the visitors, many of whom are now threatening my father, demanding that he give back all the money he has received over the past few months for *roora*. I quickly run to the sleeping hut and find my aunt slipping out of her skirt and into her jeans. She throws her sandals into her duffel bag and puts on a long-sleeved shirt. Seeing me, tears well up in her eyes.

"Kuku, I have to leave quickly before those baboons your uncles come after me. They will beat the skin off my back this night if I do not run now. I promise that one day when all this is over and forgotten, I will come back and get you out of here. Just be strong, OK? And remember that you are no one's possession to sell. If they try it, run away, you hear me? I have to get out of here now."

My aunt gives me a tight hug and sobs. I am numb and my arms remain at my side. Then, in a flash, she disappears out of the door and is gone. I see her black T-shirt, forgotten on the floor. I pick it up, put it to my face and inhale deeply, hot tears falling from my eyes. I look around the small stuffy hut and inhale the lingering scent of Impulse.

I hear her voice and her laughter: "When I walk by they will know that Christina the Colourful is on her way here, has been here or is here, somewhere, somewhere."

I am an African, am I?

Mzana Mthimkhulu

"Your white masters must be delighted with you!" Mark hissed into my ear as we filed out of the general manager's office into the wide corridor.

"What for?" I frowned, tilting my head away from his irritating voice. He caught up with me and we walked side by side. Our shoes made a swishing sound on the brown rubber-tiled floor.

"As if you don't know," Mark chuckled.

"What for?" I repeated in a raised voice.

"For being unAfrican in the way you do things. We have tolerated you being the only one at the canteen who eats *isitshwala* with fork and knife but today you outdid yourself."

It was my turn to chuckle. "Doing things in a convenient and efficient way is not a white man's preserve. I am comfortable when I eat *isitshwala* with fork and knife, not my fingers. Anyway, what crime am I supposed to have committed this time?"

"In the meeting, you hogged all the limelight for the wrong reasons."

I abruptly stopped and grabbed Mark by the wrist. The rest of the managers went past us and hurried down the staircase.

"What are you talking about?"

Mark shook his greying head. "You should have listened to yourself in there when you announced that you had not used all of your monthly fuel allocation. The pride in you voice was sickening. Worse was to come – Mr Wilson applauding you." Mark mimicked Mr Wilson's deep voice and his habit of shaking his head from side to side when talking. "Well done Tim. That is the kind of responsible behaviour I expect from my managers. In these difficult times, conserving fuel is a service not only to the company but also

21

to the country as a whole. Fuel is foreign currency and foreign currency is to a modern economy what oxygen is to a living thing."

Mark shook his head again and sighed. Now speaking in his normal voice, he continued, "No doubt, you can't wait to assemble the wife and kids at home to tell them what a good African boy you have been. I suppose congratulations are in order – well done Uncle Tom. From now on you are an honorary white." He freed himself from my grip and softly clapped in front of my face.

I grabbed his wrist again and dragged him down the steps. We swept past the switchboard pair at reception and walked into the ground floor corridor. Ignoring his protests, I pushed him into my office and closed the door behind me. A couple of telephone messages were on my neat desk calendar but I had a more urgent matter to deal with.

"Listen Mark," I growled, wagging a threatening finger.

"There you go. You know my real name is Makaziwe – a name with historical significance and meaning to my family and me. Every self-respecting African attaches importance to our traditional names but not Timothy Mdlongwa. Like your white masters, you find it a chore to pronounce African names, so you just rename me Mark."

I clicked my tongue in annoyance. "Don't run away from the issue and try to hide behind that student union radicalism. The issue here is behaving responsibly. There is nothing unAfrican about me only using the quantity of fuel I need to. The trouble with you and your kind is that you see racism under every desk and chair. In the process you conveniently dismiss responsible behaviour as unAfrican."

Hands thrust in his trouser pockets, his beer belly hanging, Mark gave me a pitying look. He sadly shook his head and sighed. "Don't you have relatives in the townships and in the rural areas?"

"Of course I do," I snapped. "But what has that got to do with-"

"Everything," he shouted, swinging his hand like a demagogue addressing a rally. "A true African visits relatives as a matter of routine. No son of the soil ever fails to use up all his fuel allocation. Obviously, you do not see yourself as one of us. You spend your weekends behind high walls in the leafy suburbs watching satellite TV. Then like a dog running back with the stick thrown by its master, you come wagging your tail – 'master, unlike these other managers, I have conserved your precious fuel.'"

I snorted. "I suppose driving to a bottle-store 40 kilometres away from the city and then *braaing* steak and sausages with your small house as you often do is the proper African way of spending weekends?"

Mark scowled and peered past the Venetian blinds. A truckload of coal slowly drove past. After a few seconds of silence, Mark turned round to glare at me. "Very unlike you who spends your weekends reclining on the sofa and listening to Mozart?"

"You know I cannot tell Mozart from... who is the other one... Beethoven. Reggae is my music. Is that also unAfrican?"

The small house jibe had deflated Mark. I could see he had no desire to continue the argument. Rumour had it that his latest small house was the vivacious girl in accounts. "I am expecting a visitor in a few minutes," Mark claimed.

"Let us finish what you started," I fumed. "Is having an affair with a subordinate the mark of a true son of the soil?" Mark was out of the office before I finished the sentence.

I sat at my desk to work. Try as hard as I could to concentrate, Mark's criticism gnawed at me. Was I not a true African? Had I sold out? True, I had not visited a relative in the previous two months. How could I when I had been busy? Busy doing what? Well, the economy was in a mess and this turned my job as purchasing manager into a nightmare. In spite of the cash flow problem and that of a nationwide shortage of almost every item the company needed, I was expected to buy all requirements on time. Impatient colleagues virtually camped in my office, chasing me to chase their urgent orders. Chasing me, as if I was a rabbit and they were hounds.

As a child, a myriad of taboos were drilled into me. Never walk backwards, for your mother will fall into a calabash. Sit not on a road or path, for boils will grow on your buttocks. Woe unto those who whistle in the house, for snakes will rush in. Now an adult and working at a beer brewing company, one taboo reigned – never do, or omit doing something that will result in the factory stopping.

Instant dismissal awaits those who flout this taboo. Day and night, weekend and public holidays, I was kept on my toes to ensure that the company machines kept turning.

Was it a sin then that on Saturday afternoons, I relaxed by playing golf with friends at an exclusive club? Afterwards, we would banter over drinks. Who in my profession does not know the importance of networking with suppliers and transporters?

With all due respect to my relatives, which one of them could give me tips on how to survive in this hostile work environment? My mind raced back a year when I last attended our monthly family burial society gathering at Aunt's place. The meeting was supposed to start at two but there we were, only three of us at two thirty waiting for about fifteen more to arrive. We sat on the vinyl sofas in the sitting room while Aunt prepared soft drinks in the kitchen.

"Looks like we are in for another drought," my cousin Zamani moaned soon after we completed the long process of greeting each other. "January is almost over yet we have now gone for three weeks without a single drop of rain." I nodded, understanding how he felt. As soon as his factory went on shutdown last December, he rushed home to oversee the ploughing and planting of the crops. By early January, his wife and children had planted forty kilograms of maize seed and several other crops. Reports were now coming in that, because of the continuing drought, crops across the country were wilting. Poor Zamani was picturing the sorry sight of his crops. He shook his head and repeated, "not a single drop of rain."

"And we have no one to blame for that but ourselves," Uncle Nqabeni declared, jabbing the air with his finger. "You all know me, I am Joshua Nkomo's number one supporter but I do not mince my words about when the old man blundered. Nkomo made a mistake when he and his victorious troops returned from Zambia. Instead of taking elderly traditional leaders to the Njelele Shrine, he took along his young struggle heroes. Obviously, this annoyed our ancestral spirits. Even in the olden times, warriors were never more important than elders. We will never enjoy good rains until the Njelele blunder is corrected."

"Exactly," Zamani nodded. "Tradition must be observed. As if that blunder was not enough, we continue to insult the spirits of our ancestors. With their mini-skirts and sweatshirts, our young women now roam the streets almost naked. Some go for those tight fitting hipsters."

"Do not limit your criticisms to women only," Aunt said as she walked in with a tray of drinks. "What about men who go out with girls young enough to be their daughters?"

"Married men fondling their young sisters-in-law so as to speed up their ripening into mature women is part of our culture," Nqabeni chuckled. "We even have a word for it – *ukulamuza*. The only requirement is that the man supports the sisters-in-law in all their needs. So, there is nothing wrong with a generous man dating girls young enough to be his daughters. He is merely preparing them to be proper wives and at the same time distributing his riches. I am sure the ancestral spirits do not mind that. What is not

24

traditional though is for young men to plait their hair. We must do things the right way if we are to enjoy good rains."

"And you wonder why God is punishing us with successive droughts!" Aunt fumed. The men laughed.

I cleared my throat to speak. "I am sure our country is going through major climatic changes, as in the rest of the world."

"What changes?" they all asked me.

"Plenty, depending where in the world you are. Rising temperatures, less rainfall, floods and severe droughts."

Zamani snorted. "Assuming that such changes are indeed taking place, the question is what is causing them?"

"Scientists believe that a lot of it is caused by human activities such as too much cutting down of trees, the burning of coal, oil and natural gas and by veld fires. The result is that a layer of gases from these activities forms in the atmosphere and stops heat from escaping."

Zamani shook his head in amazement. "Surely you do not believe that?"

"Some of what Tim is saying is true," Uncle Nqabeni said slowly. "I agree that climate changes are occurring throughout the world and I am sure these are caused by human activities. My niece Khathazile phoned me from London the other day. She said for the past five years, each winter has been colder than the previous one. As I speak, they are going through the coldest January in fifty years. That's climate change for you. She also said in the evenings she exercised in a gym that used to be a church. What is wrong with those Londoners? How can they turn a house of God into a sports centre? It is such things that are causing climate changes. People everywhere are no longer following their religions and traditions. God is obviously angry-"

"Uncle," I interrupted, "there is sufficient scientific evidence to show that…" My voice was drowned by the laughter from all three.

"Grow up Timothy," Zamani said, "we are not in a science class. The truth is, there is no mysterious layer of gases forming up there."

I tried to put my points across but whatever I said confirmed the view that I was a dreamer.

Recalling all this, I clicked my tongue sitting at my desk. These were the people who Mark wants me to spend more time with. Why waste time thinking about the views of that village idiot called Mark? I had some machine bearings to chase.

I phoned Sandra at City Bearings to find out the latest on the bearings that she kept promising me. "Did you not get my telephone message?" an excited Sandra asked. "I have your bearings and was about to leave for a supermarket where I have been promised five 10 kilogram bags of mealie-meal. It's more than my requirements. Would you want a couple at the controlled price?"

"Sure," I said just to please her. Although mealie-meal was in short supply, I had hoarded enough to last my family two months.

An hour later, Sandra personally delivered the bearings and two bags of mealie-meal. To circumvent the long security arrangements, I met her at the parking bay. After small talk, I opened the small box of bearings and checked the contents. I nodded in satisfaction and then threw the two bags of mealie-meal into the boot of my Mazda 626.

Mealie-meal goes bad within three months, I thought as I walked back to my office. Besides, even though *isitshwala* is often touted as the true African dish, I am not crazy about that sticky, tasteless maize-meal product. Suddenly, guilt assailed me. Mark would cite my lack of love for *isitshwala* as further evidence of my unAfricanness.

In a flash, I knew what I had to do to convince Mark and perhaps myself that I was a true African. I swirled round at the security gate and headed back to my car. Ten minutes later, I was driving past Mpopoma Total towards Pumula Township. It was months since I had driven in the townships. The vibrancy around me was a refreshing change from the dullness of the suburbs. In spite of the fuel shortage, traffic was busy. School children in uniforms were walking in all directions. Churchwomen in various denominational uniforms reminded me that it was Thursday.

My aunt was tilling the flower garden when I parked in front of her house. She straightened up slowly to her imposing height. Worry increased the wrinkles on her narrow face as she approached me.

"Everything all right?" she asked, opening the chest-high gate.

"Perfect," I smiled.

She chuckled in disbelief. "Then where did I bath this morning to be honoured with a visit by the high and mighty? Seriously, what brings you here?"

"Nothing," I stressed, as though hurt by her question. "I was missing you and so here I am." I flung out my hands in a way that said I am all yours.

"How thoughtful of you," she said, shaking my hand but eyeing me with suspicion. I walked behind her on the brick paved path to the back of the house. Through the kitchen, she led me to the sitting room. Now seated on a sofa, I asked her how some of our relatives were. She enjoyed updating me on the latest developments of the Mdlongwa family. At a quarter to two, a colleague phoned me on the cell to remind me about a meeting at two.

"I can't make it," I told him. "I am seeing an important supplier."

"But...."

"No buts, I could be coming back with the bearings you guys are crying for."

Eyebrows raised, Aunt asked me as soon as I switched off, "So now I am an important supplier?"

"Yes. You are supplying important news about my family. Without you guys, what am I? Nothing."

Aunt looked at me with a mixture of surprise and approval. "If you want more news, come here next Saturday afternoon for the monthly meeting of the family burial society. It's months since you attended one."

I ignored the admonishing tone and we chattered some more before I finally bid her farewell. As we strolled to the Mazda, a short fat lady with a multi-coloured wrap-over cloth marched towards us.

"That is our gossip queen," Aunt whispered to me. "We call her Dot Com. Always sniffing around for nasty stories to tell. Hello girl," Aunt shouted in a cheerful voice when Dot Com got near.

"Is everything all right?" Dot Com asked in a concerned voice.

A smug smile brightened Aunt's face. "Things have never been better."

"Then why the long visit?" she queried, glancing at me.

"Oh that," Aunt laughed, waving her hand. "We the Mdlongwas visit each other just to keep in touch."

"Is that so?" Dot Com grunted. She tried to hang around, but Aunt told her we had some family business to conclude.

"You have made my day!" Aunt exclaimed as soon as Dot Com left. "How many times in this neighbourhood do executive cars park at a house when there is neither an important message being delivered nor a function going on?"

I walked round to the back of the car, opened the boot and lifted out one 10 kilogram bag of mealie-meal. "Have this," I said. For a moment, Aunt was speechless.

"Son of my brother," she finally said, "the spirits of our ancestors must have spoken to you and sent you here. Do you know that we have gone for four days, *four days* without *isitshwala*?" She sighed. "Only God will know how to thank you enough for me."

I hurried into the car before the gathering tears in her eyes fell down. After mumbling a farewell, I drove off.

Now on the road, I fell back on the seat and roared, "Talk to me, Makaziwe. The spirits of my ancestors have spoken to me, my aunt is proud of me, come Saturday afternoon, instead of going to the golf club, I will be attending a family gathering – am I not a true African?"

Making a Woman

Thabisani Ndlovu

Skhumba is trying to say to Aunt Mongi, he cannot sleep at night because he loves her. Grown-ups can say stupid things like that and their eyes tell you these are useless things. Look at Skhumba's eyes. They are naturally small as a porcupine's and always slide away from everyone's like those of a thieving dog and now they are small small slits. And people say women die for Skhumba and some even scratch and bite each other over him. A man with a bull-frog nose like this, and smelling like a billy goat! His hands move hesitantly as he tries again. He gets the signs wrong and it comes out as *I love sleep.* With open palms facing the blue blue sky, Aunt Mongi is asking, *So?* "Tell her," Skhumba says to me, "that she has the most amazing figure I have ever seen and that everyone in Janke District is saying that. Unlike some men who think she is cursed, I don't think so. Even if she is, I don't care. Tell her she is my honey from the *mbondo* tree. I can't eat when I think of her. My heart is burning and only she can cool it."

Skhumba is asking for too much. I only spend time with Aunt Mongi during the school holidays. How does he expect me to say 'cursed'? And 'his burning heart'? This Skhumba thinks he is clever, speaking so much gibberish through his teeth that make him look as if he has been eating brown mud because he smokes newspaper-rolled cigarettes. When a man says these kinds of sweet-sweet things, closing his eyes like that and talking softly as if talking to a sick person lying on a hospital bed, he just wants to put his thing inside the woman's. I know that. So I point to Skhumba and Aunt Mongi, and show the thumb of my right hand sticking out between the cleavage of the forefinger and second finger. How the cooking stick finds Skhumba's head, I

29

don't know. I just see its broken flat end rolling briefly in the sand, the white of cooking *isitshwala* barely visible through the overall brown of sand grains. Aunt Mongi is chasing Skhumba and whacking the back of his head. Many blows rain on him and he bawls like a boy. He should have known that Aunt Mongi used to herd cattle and she is tough and fast. She is a woman now, Grandpa says, she must not do that anymore. Now she does a lot of cooking for everyone, especially Grandpa who likes her cooking. When she kneels in front of him, offering him food, a smile is always twitching at the corners of her mouth. Later, when we are alone, she caresses her chin and points at her chest, repeatedly makes the sign for eating and getting fat and laughs. Grandpa and I make a good match and she throws her head back and laughs till tears sparkle in her eyes. But she must start cooking for her own man, Grandpa says. What use will it be if she continues cooking for him until her hair turns white? There are two men who want Aunt Mongi. There is this Skhumba who is so liked by women in spite of his squashed nose and terrible smell. Women are strange. Then there is Jamu. What else can you expect from Jamu? His head is full of scorpions.

I laugh at Skhumba until I cry. When Aunt Mongi returns, I'm still laughing. She wags the stick at me and makes as if to beat me. I raise my hands in mock fear and protection of my face. She points at me and makes circles with her index finger pointing at her head, *You're just as mad.* I nod my head. She makes as if to beat me again and she laughs her white buck teeth. We laugh until she hugs me, then acts out how she beat Skhumba and how he ran, with his heels almost touching the back of his head. I roll on the sand and when I'm nearly dead with laughter, Mother comes out of the kitchen hut and says, "Hey you two, leave some laughter for some of us." Facing Aunt Mongi, Mother does the both-palms skywards, *What is it?* Aunt Mongi just waves Mother and her question away, looking aside, *Nothing and nothing you need to know.*

That Skhumba, serves him right. He will stop this nonsense talk of his. "*There* is a woman," he always says of Aunt Mongi, "she makes me soil all my trousers." Some men laugh and one of them says, "You Skhumba, that thing of yours is too greedy. Now you want *this* woman. She makes all our things stand but who are you to try her? Be careful what you ask for. You think that kind of body, that could make some of us kill our mothers for, comes on its own? So you want to lift a *mamba* to see how many young she has hatched? Good luck."

"Women," Grandpa says and shakes his head. "You know that

underneath your grandmother's *doek* is white hair?" It is one of those questions he asks without asking. Look at how he is picking his teeth, looking away from me so that he does not even see me nod. He spits out whatever piece was trapped between his teeth, which are becoming fewer and fewer. His cheeks are falling into his mouth and soon they will be so close they'll say good morning to each other. "You would think she knows better, heh? Not at all. Here she is pretending she can't see that your aunt needs help." Something is pricking me to ask him, "Help with what?" Before I decide whether he is still talking to himself he says, "Your Aunt Mongi needs to become a woman before it's too late. As God's own creature, she does." People say that of Aunt Mongi, "Agh... shame. She is God's own creature. But what a body that woman has. How many women look like that? For sure, God can't give you everything." Grandpa looks at me with his cloudy eyes and I nod. He squints more and more these days and the whitish clouds in his eyes are spreading fast. It is good to sit on the stool that Grandpa carved for me three days ago. It is a smaller version of his. On the wood supporting the seat and base are three snakes coiled around each other, their heads in whispering distance. "Son of my son," he said when he gave me the stool, "you are my first-born's son and I praise God and the ancestors that you are a boy. You will be the father of everyone here one day. See these snakes? They speak of us and those gone before us. Come sit and eat with me and learn to become a proper man." We eat a lot of meat.

Tomorrow, Grandpa is saying, we will go looking for more herbs. For now, can I drink this? He is like that. His talk jumps all over the place like a grasshopper. It is a dark-brown and slimy liquid that he gives me. Not as bitter as the one he gave me yesterday. "Makes your joints, sinews and bones strong, this one. And when it's time to father children," he makes a sharp tek sound between thumb and middle finger, "one time. You must become strong, son of my son. Very soon, you will have a beard around your thing. Give me the bottle." He gulps all that is left and says ahh as if he has taken something nice, like those people who drink Coca-Cola on tv. There at the bottom of the transparent cooking oil bottle are several little bulbs cut in half, on top of which is a green weed. He has many of these bottles and others with paws, heads, tails and guts of little creatures and people come from far away to get the medicines. Some come walking with their legs far apart. That's pain from the disease that eats their things, Grandpa says. That is why he has many cattle. Some people who would have come walking with their legs far apart come back walking properly and bring a beast or two. Some come to thank

Grandpa for making them have children and some older men come back smiling like naughty school boys, to say they are men again and may bring a goat or two. Grandpa makes people happy. He makes some of them young and strong.

Aunt Mongi is frying *vetkoeks* in a pan over the fire just in front of the kitchen hut. In a reed basket next to where she is kneeling are succulent brown ones. I point at them and cup both my hands. She looks at me, smiles and wags a finger. She points at the *vetkoeks*, rapidly thrusts the bunched fingers of one hand towards her mouth, puffs her cheeks, rolls her eyes and holds her arms like brackets alongside her body. *Vetkoeks make you greedy and fat*, she is saying. But mother thinks it's the meat that Grandpa feeds me almost daily. I must learn to become *umnumzana,* he says. A *mnumzana* enjoys the fruit of his labour and sees to it that his children and grandchildren grow up to become proper people and not hollow things that are blown by the wind and laughed at by everyone, including poor and empty people. Above all, a *mnumzana* must make sure that, in his homestead, the meat of the next beast is cooked in the gravy of the last. He says there are three Ndebele Kingdoms for a man to enjoy – meat, beer and women. He asks me to repeat the kingdoms. I get the order wrong and he tells me I would not have learnt the lesson if I get the order wrong. "Women can leave you," he says, "but you're never too old for the other two. You can eat the meat of a calf and, if that fails, you can grind the meat. Do you know that?" I say no.

Aunt Mongi points at the *vetkoeks* again and spits in quick succession ptuu! ptuu! ptuu! The spitting goes with a flicking of both wrists and a sideways glance. *These things are rubbish.* Just like she says of people she doesn't like or things that don't agree with her, like cooking oil. She can cook *vetkoeks* for everyone but if she tries to eat one she vomits. Buses and cars don't agree with her either. She can't travel on them because diesel or petrol makes her sick sick. So she doesn't want to travel to town. This is how she says town: left-right control of a steering wheel that is not there and then pointing to the east, the direction of town. She went there once, before I was born, my mother says. Aunt Mongi vows she'll never travel there again; said by scooping a bit of sand on the ground, spitting into the small hollow and covering it up with the little mound of scooped sand. *Never.*

I know there are things she can say never to and mean it. Like she refused to inherit the family's *amadlozi* even though grandmother, who carries the spirits, said Aunt Mongi was chosen by the ancestors. They brewed the beer, beat the drums and danced, but there was no Aunt Mongi. She returned home three days later and nobody knew from where. But she cannot say no to just giving me one *vetkoek*. I cup my hands, bend the head to one side and wave a forefinger. *Just one please.* She laughs her white buck teeth, throws her head back, flashing her black eyes. She points at the *vetkoeks* and steadily extends the brackets of her arms. *These things will make you fatter.* She reminds me of my classmates who call me *Mafutha*. I make a sour face. She becomes soft soft, forks one *vetkoek* and gives it to me. Aunt Mongi likes me too much to say no to things like this. When I was younger, she used to carry me on her back. Now she carries Uncle Talkmore's child Sithembiso on her back.

Jamu has been here several times to talk to Aunt Mongi. He does not know how to talk to her well. He runs out of signs for what he wants to say. So I've been asked to relay his messages to Aunt Mongi when he runs out of words… signs, actually. Is this really Jamu smiling like this? Like I said, when men want to put their things inside women's, they act strangely. Which herd boy does not know the sting of Jamu's cane if the unfortunate boy's cattle graze his crops? Which herd boy can outrun Jamu except Bafana? Jamu didn't catch Bafana because he runs like a hare – round trees and shrubs, twisting and turning. Even then, Jamu took his time. Just like you leave milk to stand overnight in a gourd so the cream can rise to the top and you just scrape it off and enjoy. But for a while you forget or pretend the milk is not there and there won't be any cream. Jamu stalked Bafana for many days after the boy's escape. He caught Bafana napping under a *gonde* tree and thrashed him so much the boy peed on himself. Jamu… he doesn't play, this one. And who can complain to Jamu, eyeball to eyeball and tell him what they think except my mother? So when Jamu beat me last rainy season and the cuts from his switch made mad patterns all over my body, one of them poking my left eye, Mother got madder than the cuts and dragged me to Jamu's. "You big-boned baboon. Do you want to kill my child… eh? Why don't you have children of your own that you can murder as you please? Three women and you couldn't make them pregnant. And why did they leave you if you're the tough man you think you are? It's not my fault, you man-when-there-are-no-other-men-around. If you ever touch my child again, I'll make you see the buttocks of a snake!" Jamu just stood there, dwarfing my mother but looking as if he had been turned into a pillar of salt. Now I wonder if he ever tried any of Grandpa's medicines so he could have children.

A few days later, my father was home for the weekend, from the city where he works. When Mother told him about how Jamu had nearly killed me, asking me to remove my shirt so father could see the now not-so-mad cuts on my back, he cast one or two glances from the rim of his teacup, slurped and swallowed his tea and said, "He'll be all right. It won't kill him. That's how some of us grew up as well." Mother asked him just what the matter was with him. Was it *his* town women that were making him not care about his son? It was all right that he didn't care about her anymore. Now, his son too? Father gulped his tea, stood up without looking at Mother and went out in that Grandpa way that says "Women are mad."

In getting mad at Jamu like that, maybe Mother had forgotten that he has big fists and big boots. But my mother can get mad mad. Who doesn't know that Jamu used to work in a mine and has no shoe size that he can buy from any store. So even his mining boots, he says, had to be made especially for his big feet. The boots are so scuffed in front they show metal caps that make the boots look like mother tortoise and father tortoise whose heads are about to retreat completely into their shells. Who doesn't know that Jamu's fists have broken a lot of noses and jaws at beer drinks and his boots have broken many men's ribs? They say he has *ngoromera*, the spirit of fighting, and the main ingredient of his *ngoromera* is a blind worm from a stubborn sheep's brain. People say if you are like that, you can carry on fighting even if your arms and legs break and continue jabbing and kicking with broken limbs. You spray the person you are fighting with your bone marrow. Even if you lose both eyes, you keep fighting. That is why some people call him when they want to tame bullocks. I once saw him hold a bullock by the horn with one hand and, with the other, put a yoke over its neck. Even stubborn ones end up kneeling on their front knees, people say. But now he is smiling and asking me to tell Aunt Mongi that she will have a good life with him, that he has many cattle and she will have all the food and clothes she wants. She laughs without laughing and says she has all the food and clothes she wants. It is true that he has many cattle. So many he has no idea how many he has. Some he has loaned to poor relatives and even there, they may number fifty or so per homestead. "But he is so stingy," my mother says. "He only eats the meat of those that die suddenly or are weak from old age. God can't give you everything."

Jamu does not know what to say anymore. He walks round Aunt Mongi as she washes the dishes at the mopane table just close to the edge of the homestead to the east. He walks round her like a cock does before getting on top of a hen – spreading its wings, ruffling them against its body and hopping on one leg, making a gurgling sound that dies in the throat. His smile turns into a baring of teeth as he looks around to see if anyone is watching. He is behaving like my naughty dog Bazangenzani: quick look around before upsetting a pot with his head, a pot on the fire, helping himself to the juiciest piece of meat before quickly slinking away to wait for the meat to cool a bit. Jamu tries to hold Aunt Mongi's hand. She quickly snatches it away and jabs a finger at him, making those noises of frustration that my friend Sipho said were goat noises. I gave him a bloody mouth and he hasn't said that rot again. Jamu walks away.

Jamu is talking to Grandpa again about Aunt Mongi. "Yes, we should try," Grandpa keeps saying and Jamu nods his head. "Have you been taking what I gave you?" Grandpa asks Jamu and this time he nods his head very fast like a happy lizard. "Good," Grandpa says, and looks at me. "Son of my son, bring us salt from the kitchen." When I come out of the kitchen, I see Jamu sneaking into Aunt Mongi's hut, followed closely by Grandpa who ties the hasp of the door to the frame with a strong piece of wire. She is in there I know because when mother and others go to church every Saturday, she remains in her hut, mending clothes, cleaning her hut or just lying on her bed. Grandpa dashes back to his stool and sits like a schoolboy who does not want the teacher to see that he has just been up to mischief.

I hear her raised voice, the one that says she doesn't like what is happening and then the sound of something like a piece of clothing hitting a person or a wall. Then silence. She screams. Grandpa is just seated on his stool, taking bites of liver and chewing as if he is also listening to the taste. I run to him and dump the salt shaker in front of him. "What's Jamu doing to Aunt Mongi?" He looks at me the way blind people lift their heads in the direction of a soft-spoken person. "What did you say, son of my son?" he asks. I shout the question because I can hear some groaning now and then several thuds against the wardrobe and then against the wall. Trotting towards Aunty's hut, my idea is to rescue her. Grandpa yanks me by the hand and says, "He is making her into a woman. Come sit with me it'll be over soon…" Crash! Goes down the door to Aunt Mongi's hut. She and Jamu slide over the door like two overgrown children on a mountainside slide. She is only in her panties which are a bit torn on the side and Jamu's trousers are around his ankles. His thing is as stiff as a goat's horn. Aunt Mongi runs to the barn and hides there. Jamu quickly raises his trousers to where they should be but his horn is still stiff in there. You can see it bulging in front. His left eye is swollen. He is spitting blood and shaking his front teeth to see if they are loose.

35

Grandpa is scratching his head with a few white hairs left. If he carries on like this, he won't have any left. When Jamu starts walking towards the barn Grandpa says, "Leave her for now." Both men try to fix the door and give up. They will have to put back the frame that has come off the wall. It is leaning forward like a drunk about to fall on his face. They make the door lean against the wall, leaving a yawning gap they stare into as if it has called them rude names. Inside her hut, clothes are strewn all over, as if an angry whirlwind swept through her room. The little cupboard in which she keeps her underwear is lying on its side with its door flung wide-open as if saying "see." A bottle of Vaseline lies on its side on top of a black petticoat. Some panties and petticoats are still in a nice nice pile. Grandfather picks up her yellow dress, hands it to me and says, "Go in there and give her this dress. Tell her to come out. No one will harm her. It's for her own good." He sighs and says, "This curse of mine."

It is dark inside the barn. It was re-thatched not so long ago and still has the smell of new thatching grass and *shumba*, the green powder we add to grain so it can stay longer without being eaten by weevils. Grandma added the *shumba* a few days ago, after two or so weeks its smell will go away. Right at the end of the corridor I can make out the handlebars of an ox-drawn plough. On both sides of the corridor are small window-like openings that tell you how many compartments the barn has. I love going into the compartments to pour grain, to tread on rising piles that caress my bare feet until I reach the level of the opening. I stand still to listen. No sound. Peering through the first window is useless because it is almost full of sorghum. Aunt Mongi would not have fitted in there. The other compartment, full of maize, is not a possibility either. The third, of *rapoko*, is half full. It is her smell that makes me peer harder into this one. When she sniffles as well, I see the outline of her body. She is curled, with her head resting on her raised knees like the unborn child in our science textbooks. Throwing in the dress through the window would be rude. So I climb into the compartment. She accepts the dress and puts it next to her. When I try to hold her arm she pushes me so violently I find myself lying on my back on the sorghum. I quickly clamber out of the compartment and out of the barn.

Grandma is shouting at Grandpa outside. Jamu is gone. "So you have turned my child into a *tokoloshe* that lives in a barn? You must be happy with that."

"Lower your voice," Grandpa says.

"I'm saying get my child out of there you greedy man."

"What? You of all people calling me that? I love her, just like the rest of my children. But you, the mother, who is supposed to know better, want her to die an empty person, just a shell of a woman. Look at all our children. The boys all have their wives and children, and the girls too. All our children are married. Well, except for Sithabile who has just left her husband because of your poor teachings and her head that's full of wasps." Grandma is now standing arms akimbo, thrusting her neck forward and backwards to punctuate what she is saying. "Were you the one who got your children their husbands and wives?"

"What kind of a stupid question is that?" Grandpa asks and carries on, "They didn't need my help with that. They could hear and talk. How about this daughter of mine who has no mouth, no ears, God's own creature?"

"Didn't she say, right in front of us all that she doesn't want to be married, not to Jamu, not to any man?"

"What does she know?"

"I'm sure she knows, like I do, that all you want are Jamu's cattle." And with that Grandma turns and her skirt swishes angrily past me. She is muttering something under her breath. "Nozizwe," Grandpa shakes a finger at her fast receding back, "Watch your mouth. Don't shit with your mouth. If you have to, go to the bush." She walks more furiously, waddling on her rickety legs.

"Women," says Grandpa to me. "You see how mad your Granny is? Come sit with me under the *gonde* tree. There's a bit of meat left on the plate." I drag my feet there. The meat is catching in my throat and my eyes swing to the door of the barn so often. Grandpa's too, although he looks through the corners of his eyes.

The following day Aunt Mongi is out of the barn. Maybe she came out in the night. Maybe in the morning. I see her in the morning sweeping the yard with a branch of the *umtshekisane* tree in furious strokes. Dust billows around her and her teeth flash through dust that gets thicker and thicker the more she sweeps. She sees me. I wave hello. She stops sweeping and raises her hand as if she is waving to someone she does not quite recognise. I smile. She does not smile.

Jamu is here again and has been talking in low voices with Grandpa, my two uncles and our neighbour Timoti. This Jamu can lift a mother *mamba* to see how many little mambas have hatched from her clutch. Yes, he must try again, they all nod their heads. "I'll be very grateful," Grandpa says to Jamu and continues, "The ancestors laughed at me and gave me a disabled daughter But I don't think they can forgive me if she goes unfulfilled as a woman – if she is buried with a rat." "I know we will succeed, *Baba*," Jamu says, "*Baba* Siwalu said it should be a woman that has not known a man before and there should be something strange about her. He also gave me some herbs and I'm sure the ones you gave me, together with Siwalu's, can only mean we will succeed." Siwalu is the only other healer constantly on people's lips like Grandpa. But people say he has both good and bad medicines. He also gives women medicines that make men stupid stupid.

Just as one begins to make out the shapes of trees around the homestead and the huts in it, four men are speaking in low low voices in front of Grandpa's hut. Like hunters scared that the buck or hare might escape before they strike it, they hurry to Aunt Mongi's hut. Jamu bounces the door in with his huge shoulder. I listen so intently not to miss any sound of Aunt Mongiwa being made into a woman by Jamu. There's a brief scuffle and what sounds like one of her cardboard suitcases getting knocked over, a scream that is soon muffled and what I think is Grandpa saying, "Hold that leg." Then silence. After a while, a man groans like a bull that has been stabbed by a spear through the heart. More silence.

      The four men emerge from Aunt Mongi's hut. When they see me standing there, their eyes are slippery. They slide sideways like those of Bazangenzani caught stealing. "Why are you up so early?" Grandpa asks. I don't answer him. The well of words is dry and I walk away, refusing to see them.

This is the last school holiday this year. Mother says I should avoid going anywhere near Aunt Mongi. She has not been talking to anyone, not going to fetch water and not cooking for anyone. She talks to herself and throws objects at everyone when she is angry, even children. She keeps not only a sharp knife with her but a long sharp wire that was once one of the spokes to my father's Impala bicycle. She made a handle for the wire, Mother says.

      "What for?"

      "To keep Jamu away," Mother says. "Your aunt is now dangerous. Don't go anywhere near her."

Jamu is here. He has brought more clothes for Aunt Mongi and most of them are the big balloon type that women wear when they have a child growing inside them. "For the moment, she is as mad as a rabid dog. She won't let me come anywhere close. What kind of a daughter points both a knife and sharp spoke at her father? But once the baby is born," says Grandpa, "she will come to her senses. Don't worry Jamu." Jamu is smiling his honey-badger mouth. They say ever since he heard Aunt Mongi was pregnant, he has not fought anyone. He just drinks beer and laughs his big teeth. But Aunt Mongi does not look pregnant. Mother says she is pregnant because, when it started, she had all the signs, including throwing up in the morning.

It is a crazy crazy thing to do, going into Aunt Mongi's hut. I walk in with trembling legs, eyeing the door for a quick bolt. From the pocket of her yellow and red apron comes out the knife and long sharp wire. They wink wickedly and for a while I'm poised for a dash. When she sees it's me, she drops the two back into the pocket. She smiles a faint smile and beckons to me that I should sit down next to her. For some reason I do. She caresses my head and smiles. I point at the pocket in which the two weapons are hiding, lying against each other like good friends in doing bad. I do the palm-up, *What about those?* I add, *Do you want to kill someone?* which ends with running a forefinger across the throat. She laughs with her mouth only and shakes her head. *Are you scared of me?* she asks. I nod. She shoos my fears away and smiles.

Today I am happy. But I cannot tell Mother that I was in Aunt Mongi's hut. I can't tell Grandpa either because he might want to give me messages to take to her. Someone left the dresses that Jamu bought in her room whilst she was out. She poured paraffin on them and burnt them in the middle of the compound. There was nothing left except a little pile of soot. But now I think she is coming to her senses because here she comes with food on the big reed tray. It must be cold ox tongue and liver because that is what gets served Grandpa on the big wooden plate with a lid to it. But there is something wrong with the way Aunt Mongi is walking towards us. She walks with her legs apart like some of Grandpa's patients whose things are full of sores. Grandpa's smile grows bigger the closer Aunt Mongi approaches. Then Grandpa's smile starts vanishing like the sun behind clouds as his milky eyes also see what I see. Aunt Mongi's hands and arms are full of blood. Dark red blood covers her feet and some of it is still trickling down her left shin. She kneels in front of Grandpa and puts the tray in front of him, with traces of that smile of hers that says Grandpa likes eating too much. She gets up and leaves, walking like Grandfather's patients whose things are causing them too much pain.

When Grandpa lifts the wooden lid, there is something that looks like a big rat on the plate. Except it has two legs and a big head. It is in some water that is mixed with blood. The thing squirms for a while and is still. In front of it on the one side is the long sharp wire with a bloody handle and it looks as if it is carrying the knife on its back. I leave Grandpa like that, his mouth open as if he cannot see that flies have started settling on the big rat on his plate and might get into his mouth.

The policeman and woman ask me to say what happened yesterday. I tell them. They speak to Grandpa for a long time and for most of the time he is just shaking his head and complaining about people who make other people's matters their own. They ask him where he has put the baby. He says it was not a baby. The police say they want to see for themselves and dig up the rat-like thing, the knife and long wire with a handle from a spot next to the cattle kraal and put everything in a black plastic bag.

     The policewoman says she wants to talk to Aunt Mongi alone. Mother tells her that she only speaks through signs. The policewoman wants to know if that was Aunt Mongi's baby? Mother asks the question and Aunt Mongi nods. "How did the baby come out of her tummy?" the policewoman asks. Aunt Mongi pushes open palms in the direction of the policewoman to say, *Leave me alone.* "Ask her if she knows that she can be arrested for this?" Mother asks the question which ends with her crossing one wrist over the other. Aunt Mongi nods. "Does she understand what jail is? Does she know that she can rot in there?" the policewoman asks. Before Mother finishes asking the question, Aunt Mongi nods. Her face is very calm. Like that of someone who has walked a long distance and has since managed to sit down and have a long drink of cold water. "We will get an expert to check if her head is all right," the policewoman says and closes her small book. "She will need an interpreter. Will you do it?" she asks my mother who quickly says no, she tends to run out of signs. Mother asks if I can do it. How can I tell anything to people like these? Who are serious serious and have handcuffs dangling at their hips? I say they should ask Grandma or Grandpa, after all, they are Aunty's parents. I ask Aunt who she'd like to be her interpreter. She says I should be. The policewoman laughs without laughing and says an adult would be better. I tell Aunt Mongi, who frowns at the policewoman and signs that I'm clever and in any case, I'll be a man soon.

I don't know about all this thing of being a man soon. What I know is that I don't want to eat meat. It might be for a long long time.

Snapshots

NoViolet Bulawayo

One morning your mother reaches into the red bra she solicited from her sister Noma three years ago, and takes out a twenty. She always keeps her money in a bra so your retired father doesn't get his hands on it and send you to the store to buy two packets of Kingsgate cigarettes and therefore spend the whole day reeking of tobacco (he smokes too much). Your mother gives you the twenty and a TM Hyper plastic bag and says, You, go to Maplanka and buy one-and-a-half-white-bread-and-a-pint-of-*chimombe*.

You quickly put on your yellow *pata-patas* (which have become a little loose because your father sometimes forces his big feet into them) and *pata-pata* your way to Maplanka Store. It is about eleven minutes to get there, seven if you are sternly told to hurry, and only five-and-a-half if it's your mother that sends you. Along the way you meet Namgcobha, the bent old woman who lives in the tiny shack at the end of the block. She always wears a blood-red jersey whether it's hot or cold, and carries a clothes hanger, which you think ought to be a walking stick because every bent old person you know carries a stick and not a stupid clothes hanger.

Namgcobha quickly spies the crumpled plastic bag in your hand and says (in her thinning voice that is held together by phlegm and long pauses and hard-breathing and the stench of chewed tobacco) You, big-ass, what are you going to buy? And you say, I'm-going-to-buy-one-and-a-half-white-bread-and-a-pint-of-*chimombe*, and Namgcobha says, Only? And you nod your head and say, Yes, only, and she says, No stock margarine or sunjam or eggs or nothing? And you shake your head and say, No, no stock margarine or sunjam or eggs or nothing, mother didn't say. Namgcobha is interested in what you are going to buy because she will most likely come to your house for tea if she doesn't find anybody with better breakfast plans. You leave her muttering to herself and jabbing the air with her clothes hanger.

When you cut through the little bush right behind Maplanka you almost step on a pink used condom and you spit in revulsion; condoms are disgusting to you, but you didn't think so when you were younger. In those days you and your best friend Anesu thought condoms were really balloons, though they seemed somewhat funny shaped, and the skin, much, much thinner than regular balloons. You had no idea what the weird, smelly fluid inside those balloons was, but you merely washed them out with tap water, blew them up, tied up the opening with string and thought they made great playthings.

When your mother found you perched on the flowering jacaranda tree behind Anesu's house, playing with the condom-balloons, she climbed up after you and whooped you so much that you fell off the tree and she still whooped you and whooped you and whooped you until her red belt eventually broke. You couldn't sit for a whole two days because your buttocks were sore.

At Maplanka store, you are greeted by commotion; a mob of angry customers seems displeased with the bald-headed storekeeper and his short, pouting assistant behind the counter. You hate mobs and you don't know how you will ever negotiate your way past this one, so you just wait there by the door and try not to look at the crippled newspaper vendor who wags his red tongue (it's red because he's eating a red-mouth sherbet) at you. He does it every time and you don't know what it means but for some reason it strikes you as obscene and you wish he didn't do it.

You look down at the vendor's newspapers (so you don't have to see his disgusting red tongue) and you just keep your eyes there and read the large, black letters on the front page over and over again until you have almost memorized the words, Sudden Inflation Rocks the Country. You know what all the other words mean but you don't know anything about the word between Sudden and Rocks because it's a big word; maybe when you get to grade 6 or 7, or even to secondary school, you'll know.

When some of the angry people eventually filter out of the store (because Maplanka has threatened to call the police) you thankfully proceed to the front. You stand on tiptoe and put your damp, folded money on the peeling counter and say, in your loudest voice, mother-said-to-buy-one-and-half-white-brrr-. Before you even finish your sentence, Maplanka, the big,

43

brown storekeeper, tells you in a growling voice that your money is not enough. He says that the price of bread and milk and everything else has gone up and you need a whole lot more.

Still, you wait for Maplanka to take your money and give you your things and your change because you know you bought the same things with a twenty yesterday, so how can you not buy the same things with the same twenty today? You remain standing there, on one leg like a cock, because somehow you are convinced Maplanka is playing with you but no, he is not playing because he picks your money, flings it to your face and tells you to either go wipe your ass with it, or get some more, and to tell your mother to read what he calls, the fackeny newspapers. How does he know it's your mother who sent you and not your father? And what is there to read in the newspapers? And why are they fackeny?

When your mother sees you without the tea things she stands up from scrubbing the floor, her large hands on her exploding hips and barks, You, black-face, did you lose my money? You look down at her yellow polka-dotted skirt that is tucked in at the sides, the front hem partly wet from the dirty scrubbing water, and your eyes travel down the two large black circles that are also her knees. They are darkened by all those years of kneeling to scrub the floor and apply Cobra polish, or kneeling by the fire to light it up. Her knees have become two black moons.

You are still lost in your mother's moons when she thunders, I said what did you do with my money, heh? Her tone makes you shudder and you quickly stammer an incoherent sentence. It is only after she slaps you (three times – left cheek, pha! right cheek, pha-pha!) that you finally tell her clearly that Maplanka said the money is not enough. You leave the part about reading the fackeny newspapers.

What do you mean my money is not enough? Are you mad? A twenty, heh? A twenty, twenty, twenty! You blink away hot tears and look at your mother's two fingers, raised in front of your face to emphasize twentiness. Without opening her mouth, your mother tells you to stay where you are and boils into her bedroom, slamming the door shut behind her. When she spews out a few minutes later, she has tied a red rag over her head that matches the black widows in her eyes, and is wearing your father's black moccasins that are large for her feet. She tells you (without opening her mouth again) let's go, and you follow behind like a tail, your *pata-patas* making rapid pata-pata-pata sounds that make you uncomfortable.

Back at the store, Maplanka can tell, just by glimpsing the woman who charges in like a maddened bull, that one does not grab your mother by the horns like he does with everybody else. He quickly walks around the counter and shakes her hand. Before she even opens her mouth, he tells her (in a voice much, much lower and nicer than the one he used with you) that overnight the government has hiked prices of food and fuel and everything else, and he points to the newspaper vendor and adds, It's all in the papers.

Maplanka says, It's all in the papers, as if those papers actually have a voice with which they can shout, Yes it's true-it's true-it's true! Your mother opens her mouth, maybe to vomit, You lying bastard, like she is most likely to do in such a situation, but before she can say it, Maplanka adds, What's worse, is that this is only the beginning. What is coming for this country is even bigger than Jesus' father himself.

And that is only the beginning of things falling apart. Within a short while, prices soar even higher and it is difficult to afford anything. Commodities disappear from Maplanka's shelves and the shelves of other stores and before you know it, stores are just stores by name because they are empty It becomes pointless to even go to the store because what will you buy there, and with what money?

The water and electricity are cut off at different times of the day so you need to keep your drinking water in a big *nkonxa* and take your showers early and fast. On TV, the beautiful white man with the woman's hair (the one who can't quite say Zimbabwe and says Zeembaymbey) comes on all the time and says, thih whorl cowntry ohf Zeembaymbey eaze fowrced toh tayk drahstic steyps toh conseyrve pohwer aynd ihts seetyzens kneeyd toh cohperate. You listen to him and wonder, what really is pohwer? Isn't it what is used to beat somebody up? What is a whorl cowntry? Is there a half-cowntry somewhere?

You and your sister Rose have to stop going to school because school fees are suddenly so expensive, so it's just your brother Vulindlela who goes. Your father says it's best to send Vu to school because he is a boy. He will take care of the family once he finishes, not like you and Rose who are girls and will one day go off to get married and make some man and his clan better with your education that they didn't even pay for. When your father says this, you want to ask him how Vu will help the family since he is a serious dunderhead who always comes last in class, but you just keep quiet because you can't ask your father questions that will make him look wrong.

Vu doesn't get to go to school for long after all, because he eventually runs away with his friends, Khuluza and Mafana and Bhari, and they cross the border to South Africa. Everybody is suddenly moving to South Africa. He leaves a letter promising to return when things get better, but you and Rose cry because it feels empty without him. Now who will beat that ugly Jabu, for saying, pssssssssst, hey sexseeeeeey, when you walk past his house? Your mother sheds tears because her child is gone and she wonders how he will survive in a foreign land; everybody knows South Africa is dangerous, don't they say that yellow-skinned young man, Bigboy, was flung out of the window of a flat in that very South Africa, and wasn't Madlamini's son Tichaona shot in the head over there?

Your father doesn't cry for Vu, maybe because it is taboo for a man to cry, what on earth will people say when they see a grown man's tears? Instead, he keeps his face intact like a newly-knit red jersey and tolerates the news without showing even a wince. When his face eventually moves, it is only to blow out the thick, smelly smoke from the paw-paw cigars, and to bite his bottom lip in the teaspoon-sized hope that his only son will make it, and if Vu makes it, he might send some Pall Mall cigarettes from that South Africa.

What your father doesn't know is that there won't be Pall Malls. Shortly after the man who smuggles Vu and his friends into South Africa leaves them on the pulsating streets, and before Vu has even gotten used to the new air coursing in his lungs, he will suffer seven stab wounds by a group of impatient, unsmiling youths who are tired of people like Vu just coming to their country and taking over things. They will leave him lying there on the street, life crawling out of his body the way air reluctantly leaves a punctured condom. And when the bow-legged policeman who finds Vu clinging to his life asks him who he is and where he is from, all Vu will manage to say is the word, Zeembaymbey, as he chokes on his blood. Unknown and his body unclaimed, he will be buried in a mass grave along with other nameless people.

Your father wakes up every morning and says again and again, fack the fackin' gavment, mostly because he hates smoking the paw-paw leaves. Your mother thinks it's a good thing that he can't afford cigarettes any more because that means he might finally get better after all. The smoking gives him an awful cough and even though your mother complains, he just laughs and smokes some more. Your mother hopes that without the Kingsgates the

46

cough will go away just like a terrible vulture will seek new earths once carrion ceases to fall. What she doesn't know is that the cough has a name and that name is lung cancer and that cancer has already ravaged your father's lungs and liver and pelvis and whatever else there is to ravage in there, and so his not smoking won't help any.

The nurses are on strike when the lurking snake that is your father's lung cancer finally crawls out of its dark cave, perhaps because it has devoured all there is to devour inside his body. Taken by surprise, your father quickly succumbs, like a paper in flames. A sympathetic friend of a neighbour carries your family to Mpilo hospital in a groaning, black Peugeot 404. When you get there you find such a long, writhing line; scores of people just stand there, in pain and cooking in the sun, but patient because what else can you do in a hospital line besides be in pain and cook in the sun and be patient?

You don't go into the hospital with everybody else because children are not allowed inside (why? you don't know). You stay outside and wait and wait, and after what seems like ages and when you are tired of counting the unhappy faces around you, your party at last comes out, but without your father. You think your mother's shoulders are suddenly stooped, as if she had also gone inside the hospital to find her aged self. She drags her feet in your father's moccasins and only stops briefly to look at you like she is seeing you for the first time. Her face is tired, and she doesn't tell you anything and you don't expect her to because who are you? You are just a child and grown-ups don't ever report to children.

It's Rose (who was allowed in because she is tall and has breasts even though she is just Rose and not an adult) who whispers that your father was ADmitted. She also adds, with an air of relished importance, that they put him on a DRip and OXygen. You are jealous of Rose because she gets to stand there and use grown up words while you keep your mouth shut and listen like a child. You wish you had been allowed in, not so you could see your father (because you have lived with him all your life and know exactly what he looks and smells like) but only so you could look at the DRip and OXygen. What will you say you saw at the hospital when Anesu and your other friends ask you? You tell yourself that on the next visit you will beg to be allowed inside, just for once, so you can look.

You will never get to see what DRip and OXygen look like after all because your father dies sometime in the long, unmoving night. There is a sudden electricity cut and because the hospital is too poor to afford a generator or power back-up, there is nothing to do about the DRip and

47

OXygen that is trying to keep your father alive. There is also nobody to do nothing about anything since most of the nurses are on strike and so your father dies, life slowly whiffing out of him like braided cigarette smoke from a pack of 20 Kingsgate bought at Maplanka for $3600.

When you hear your father is dead you at first don't really know how to behave, because nobody you know has died before, and Anesu has told you almost everything there is to know about everything, except what is to be done when your own father dies. It is only when you see all the crying going on around you that you realize you are supposed to cry live tears. Your mother wails the loudest, dressed head to toe in black mourning clothes that you think very much become her brown skin. It is a new thing to see her cry like that and, somehow, you are fascinated and want to touch her tears. You look at her and ask yourself, do the tears of a tall woman who has hips that explode and black moons on her knees and fire in her eyes and thunder in her voice, have the same texture as the tears you shed after she whoops you with her red leather belt?

Rose is busy crying too, and you think she appears important, her head covered in a black, mourning scarf and looking almost like a woman. Why didn't she get you a scarf so you could look like a woman too? You also wonder what your brother Vulindlela would do if he were here, what would Vu do? Would he really cry, and would he cry like a man, and how do men cry since they are not allowed to shed tears?

Many of your relatives come for your father's funeral, some you know, some you don't know, and some you like, some you don't like. Funerals usually take three or four days but your father's takes only one day because what will the mourners eat? Plus, there is not enough water and electricity to have a regular funeral. Your relatives put their money together and buy your father a brown pine coffin. You aren't supposed to see dead people because you are a child but then they forget to tell you and Rose not to come in when all the adults are filing into the sitting room for body viewing. You stand at the back of the line and follow everybody else to look.

You have never seen your father look like this and seeing him lying there, dressed as if he is going somewhere important, like a wedding, you realize that he is a beautiful man. His face is still and relaxed, no creases from worrying about where he will get his Kingsgates and with what money, and his lips for once are sealed and not half open to let out cigarette smoke.

When everybody has gone back to wherever they came from, except the male relatives from your father's side of the family, you are suddenly afraid. Maybe it's because they have those stern faces that refuse to smile. They discuss your father's death, which to them is suspicious because how can he, SaVu, die so young, not even fifty, how could that happen? There is no logical explanation except the one they know between themselves, and so it is decided that your mother must leave; she was a bad wife and bad mother after all, look now, where is the sole heir? Didn't she chase him away to South Africa so she can inherit the house after her husband died of the *muti* she was mixing with his food?

Your mother is told to pack her bags and leave the house because your Uncle Mandla, your father's youngest brother, will soon be moving in as is the custom. You and Rose (who are staying because who doesn't know the children belong to the man's family?) stand by the window, looking and listening as your mother's fate is being discussed. You can see your mother, seated there on the floor with her head bent and looking like a setting sun, facing all those men who are seated on chairs and looking important. They are your grandfather, your father's brothers and his cousins and some of them you don't really know.

The sun is ravishing the red earth when your mother carries her black suitcase on her head and walks out of the house like a bad disease. She is also walking out of her history, which is this: she has woken up every day around six in the morning and swept the floors of the house and scrubbed them with a wet cloth and applied black Cobra polish and then shined the floor on her knees before going out to sweep the yard. She has cooked meals every day in the kitchen and sprinkled holy water on the walls of the house each night before going to bed. She has brought up all her three children within those walls, and knelt on the floor everyday to hold the dish for her husband (whose smoking she did not like) so he could wash his hands before taking the meals she has prepared, and she has also counted her blessings and fears and hopes and dreams in that house.

This is your mother's history, but it doesn't matter now since she is walking out of it because it is all tied to a house that was never hers to begin with. That day you will also learn, without being told, that women come from their fathers' houses to live in their husbands' houses. They claim nothing, just like the sun that daily descends to warm and caress and enliven, only to go back to its mother as naked as it came, with not even a token of thank you. Uncle Mandla is standing there by the door to make sure that your mother doesn't try to sneak away with either a token or a part of her history because he knows that a woman with her large breasts can sneak something in her bra.

You stand by the window and watch your mother walk out of the yard and down the dusty Sibhizi road, not even turning once to wave or to take a last look at what has been her home for all these years. When she eventually disappears from sight you run to look at yourself in the mirror and you realize that you actually look like your father. You also look like Uncle Mandla and your other uncles and your grandfather and you don't look anything like your mother at all.

You comfort yourself with the promise that one day, when you grow up, you will find your mother and go and live with her. With this promise you bite your bottom lip with something that resembles hope because at least you will get to see your mother again. You will pull the thin, grey blanket over your head and try to sleep but you won't because you will dream of your father calling you from under the earth to bring his cigarettes.

Years later you will seek out your mother and will be so happy to see her after so long a time, but she will welcome you with the thick restraint of a stranger. She will be wearing her new husband's moccasins (that fit her better than your father's) and talking to her new children in a new voice. You will look at those children, a naughty boy named Tawanda and a shy little girl named Thandiwe, and you will envy them your mother and hate them for stealing her.

Your mother will tell her new husband that you are her niece and he will greet you with a smile bandaged with cigarette smoke, but will not even ask your name. And when you and your mother are finally alone she will tell you, in a gentle voice you can't recall from before, that she cannot be your mother anymore. She will tell you she is now another man's wife and that man will not have another man's children in his home. Finally she will walk you to the gate, holding your hand tight like the first day she took you to crèche and watch you get on the bus after asking you to please stay away please.

You are fourteen-and-a-half when you meet Givemore on Main Street. You are selling hard boiled eggs from a white hand-dish that you balance effortlessly on your head as you sashay down the pavements, almost like a woman, sometimes singing, eggs-eggs-eggs-eggs-eggs or simply hissing, kssssssssssss, to attract attention to your wares. At first you didn't even like selling, but that was the only thing left to do since Uncle Mandla didn't buy enough food; he just bought beer and more beer and so you ended up having to sell to survive.

You are walking down Seventh Avenue, stopping every now and then to admire the clothes that are displayed within shop windows, mannequins in all sorts and sorts of styles. When you were little and you came to town with your mother you used to smile and wave at the mannequins because you thought they were people.

Now that you are grown, you don't wave, you only look at the clothes and wonder when you will ever afford to buy new clothes again. Maybe it's a good thing that Rose ran away from home (because she said Uncle Mandla was trying to do bad things to her) and followed Vu to South Africa, leaving most of her clothes behind (which you can now fit since you are taller) because otherwise what would you be wearing if that had not happened?

You are standing at a corner and admiring a white hello kitty shirt when a woman with an impatient face and a child on her back stops you and says, How much? and you tell her $1000. She reaches a hand in a red bra and searches and searches and finally pulls out a knotted white handkerchief, which she unties with her yellowish teeth. When she bends slightly to sink her teeth deeper in the fabric, you catch a glimpse of the baby on her back. Its face is calm and beautiful and has a stillness that reminds you of your father's face in the coffin.

It's the black caterpillar crawling into the baby's nose that makes you wonder why the baby is not crying, surely it must feel the insect? You are thinking of swatting the caterpillar off when the woman suddenly straightens up and the baby's face disappears and you quickly forget about it as your eyes count the bills dropping like dead fruit from the woman's hand onto your palm, $1000. You give her an egg and a pinch of salt in a folded newspaper with half the face of the country's president, and she shuffles away before you can say thank you.

You are standing there watching the woman crossing the road without even waiting for the robot to turn green, her body melting into the gushing sea of cars swerving, trying to avoid hitting her. Brakes, horns, screeching tyres, the screaming stench of rubber on tarmac. And a slicing *futseki nja mgodoyi*, I'll kill you whore! You are so nervous for her you almost drop your dish of eggs. At the same time the slick, black car pulls to a stop about a stone-throw away and a man with a bald head rolls down the window.

You don't get to the car in time because the much quicker boys appear from the shadows and beat you to it, whistling and scrambling for the man's money. You hear crowded voices cry in fierce competition, Buy my eggs! Buy my maize, straight from the farm! Puleezee boss, buy my fried fish, fresh from the skies! but the man impatiently waves the boys away.

You are surprised when the man calls out to you and beckons with a finger. You are convinced he is mistaking you for somebody else, because he calls you Sunrise. What you will soon learn is that the man is not mistaken and that he is referring to you as Sunrise because names, like eggs and salt, can be given anytime, even on the street, and by strangers. You will also learn that the man doesn't want the eggs balanced on your head (even though he will buy them all with crisp money that smells of newness) but wants other things that you don't even know you have.

Sunrise. You will find out about those other things when the man (who is old enough to be your father but insists you call him by his first name, Givemore) puts an end to your bleak career as a seller of boiled eggs. He will shower you with money and lavish you with gifts and marinade you with attention. You won't know what to do except giggle and tremble, baffled by this strange magic you never knew you had, that makes a grown man bombard you with expensive things without you even opening your mouth to utter a single word.

Sunrise. You will shed your old self like a snake sheds its skin and become something new. Givemore will remove you from the hell that is the street, with its searing sun and mean boys and smelly trash. He will rent you a room in the fancy suburb of Budapest because he is convinced that your guardian uncle (who is forever drowning in beer) will come home drunk one day and think you are not his niece but just a girl named girl.

Sunrise. The day Givemore stops calling you Sunrise, he will call you Sunset, and that will also be the day you will stop being a child. He will bring you bright red flowers and your favourite chocolate with that strange, cursived name you can't even read. You will see a man naked for the very first time, and you will tremble with awe and fear and surprise at the realization that it's true; a man has a living thing attached between the legs, there where you have nothing.

Sunset. You will watch, first with horror, and then awe, as the thing lifts like a whip and stays suspended in the air, and you will wonder if what you are seeing is real or magic. While you are still figuring it out, Givemore will insist on showing you what it is for. Being shown that is not the ordinary kind of showing, like when somebody points and says, this is a cup, spoon, stove, here is a madman, his name is Robert. Rather, it is a showing that begins with Givemore taking off your clothes and ends with you lying flat on your back, a raw, raw pain between your legs.

Sunset. The following day, Givemore gives you a huge lump-sum of money to spend. You have never seen so much money in your life, and you stare at the millions in shock because you can't even begin to think what you are going to do with it all. You feel the pain from the showing was well worth it. You are also over the moon because Givemore tells you he will be ready to marry you soon.

Sunset. You can already visualize your wedding; you will be a beautiful bride dressed in a white wedding gown with a long, long veil everyone will admire. You will prance in slippers like Sindyrella's, on a trail of red roses (even redder than Namgcobha's jersey), waltzing softly between two columns of pretty bridesmaids dressed in yellow gowns. It will be a joyous white wedding, the only sad thing will be that your mother and father and Rose and Vu will not be there to eat the rice and salad and chicken meat and drink Sprite and Fanta and beer and be proud of you.

Sunset. You are even happier to find that the times following the first time Givemore shows you what his thing is for are not as painful, and gradually, you don't even feel pain anymore. Instead, you feel a brand new pleasure. When Givemore makes you lie flat on the bed or bend over, you forget there was ever any pain associated with this in the first place. You learn to open yourself like a wound and with him panting hotly in your ear, you do whatever you think is necessary to put a smile on his creasing face.

Sunset. One day, when you are fourteen-and-three-quarter years old, after so many days of vomiting in the morning and screaming joints and nausea, you decide to go to the hospital because you can't explain your strange sickness. At first you thought it'd go away and now you are a little worried because you have always been a healthy child. You don't tell Givemore because you don't want to worry him, and something tells you he doesn't want to be worried; maybe when you become his wife you can worry him.

Sunset. It is many, many years after that day you took your father to the hospital to die and you shudder at the realization that a hospital is, after all, a place for both getting better, and for dying. You wonder, as you put on your red push-up bra, if they will also put you on a DRip and OXygen like your father, and what if, like your father, you also get ADmitted and there is a power-cut during the night?

Sunset. The little elderly nurse with a back curved almost like the hook of a clothes hanger peers at your card (she also peered at you through the window when you walked uncertainly down the corridor in your skinny jeans and low-cut tank top that vomits your cleavage). She has arranged your pregnancy test even before you knocked on the door because she could tell, just by looking at you, what you came for. She already knows exactly what she will say to you, in what words, and just with what texture of voice.

Sunset. The nurse has done this so many times before and so she knows just how much of your face the cold blanket of surprise will cover, and how shock will gradually spill over the surprise the way milk from a boiling pot spills onto burning coal. She knows you will walk out of the hospital like a zombie and, even though she is not exactly sure about when you will do what you will do when you find out, she knows you will do it.

Sunset. You are in Namgcobha's shack when you do it a week later, after hunting for her in your old neighbourhood. Finally you find her living in a place called Paradise, in a shack so tiny you have to bend to fit inside. Givemore doesn't know and you don't want him to know. Namgcobha hasn't forgotten you, after all these years, and she opens the door in a black nightdress and without even asking who it is, the way you open for Givemore sometimes because you are expecting him and you know it's nobody else but him.

Sunset. It doesn't take long for Namgcobha to prepare. There is already, spread on the floor, a grass mat that has been, and will still be used for many other things. A red candle rests on a low stool and lights up the floor. Namgcobha hands you a wire clothes hanger, which she instructs you to undo and straighten and you comply, wondering, as you feel the wire struggle for life in your hands, why you have to straighten the thing because you don't see what it can possibly be used for under the circumstances, but you don't ask because some things you just can't ask.

Sunset. Once you have the hanger straightened you place it on the mat besides the other things Namgcobha has lined up. A little dish with detergent in it, a rag, a towel, a sponge, and some things you don't even know, but still, you don't ask. When she says, you take off your skinny jeans and underwear and lie on your back on the mat, legs spread apart, feet touching the floor.

Jab jab jab jab jab jab jab jab jab jab jab jab jab jab jab jab jab jab jab jab jab jab jab jab jab jab jab jab jab jab jab jab jab jab jab jab jab jab

jab jab...

Sunset. The next time that you are with Givemore after the clothes hanger incident, and you have used the herbs Namgcobha gave you to use and got rested, you love him with a murderous tenderness. You feel him deep inside you and squeeze him hard, grateful his thing is not a jabbing wire but something that offers a dizzying sweetness. You hold him real tttttttttttttight, your legs coiled around his waist like a snake. Before he leaves, he promises you a new car of your choice and you smile a star, already thinking of the long and short and fast and slow journeys you will make, though you know fully well that you aren't even old enough to drive.

Sunset. That night you will sleep on your left side, your curved elbow neatly tucked under your head and count all the blessings you have and look forward to those that you feel are coming. What you won't know is that those blessings that are yet to come will not matter. During your sleep, the walls of your womb will groan and shake and fall apart. You will gush thick and dark, endless blood, and when you reach down under there you will find part of an intestine dangling. When they take your body away in the morning you will leave, there on the bed, a sunset-coloured stain the weight of cigarette smoke.

Her Skin is a Map

Raisedon Baya

The park has changed. The grass is no longer entwined together like lovers. The green is gone, replaced by an angry gold that attacks the eyes. The trees look unhappy, betrayed. If they could walk they would have left the park a long time ago.

My earliest memory of the park goes back thirty years – a lifetime in Zimbabwe. I was five years old and had come to the park for a family picnic. We were a small family then. My parents were young, with just three children and the whole future before them. The family has since grown. Mother has six grandchildren now. Father is late and Mother now lives in the rural areas. She is much happier there, surrounded by nature. But my guess is that the real reason she is there is that she wants to be near Father, who is buried there.

I still remember the picnic because it was one of the few occasions we gathered together as a family just to have fun. We had rice and chicken, slices of cake, sweets and strawberry ice cream. It was like Christmas. Father had cold beer. He brought several bottles nicely wrapped in newspaper to keep them cold, and to keep them hidden. Public drinking is a crime in Zimbabwe. I don't remember if Mother drank or whether she even ate anything. She was all over. I remember her laughing and smiling.

After the rice and chicken, I wandered through the park with my two brothers. The park seemed immense, big enough to get lost in. Our first port of call was the pond with its brightly coloured fish. We stood at the edge and threw pieces of cake into the water, watching the fish scramble for the food. I remember throwing a five cent coin into the water and making a wish to travel around the world. I haven't travelled as much as I wished but my

56

writing has reached into many corners.

The pond had a fountain that spat mouthfuls of water into the sky and then seemed to swallow them as they came down. Excited, we took off our shirts, allowing the water to fall onto our dark bodies. When the water leapt towards the sky it painted a spectrum in the air. "Look, a rainbow!" I yelled at my brothers and the three of us joined hands and each made a wish.

"I wish to be rich and have a park as big as this one to myself," Ndaba said. He is the dreamer in our family.

"I want to get married to the most beautiful woman." This from Ruvengo who was twelve and loved talking about love and women. I doubt very much if he knew the true meaning of love then. Years later, he got what he had wished for. He married a beautiful woman but it did not last.

"I wish I had wings to fly wherever I choose to go" I said and began to sing:

> If I was a bird
> And had wings
> I would fly
> High into the sky
> Bru –u –u – u
> I would fly away

The fountain rained on us as we screamed in excitement. When Mother saw us without shirts, dripping wet, she yelled, "Guys, get dressed. We don't want you catching pneumonia. Ruvengo *iwe!*..." We didn't let her finish as we ran towards the bird sanctuary. The park was a place of colour and we sped past beds of flowers.

We called the guards green men and one watched us as we approached the sanctuary. The birds saw us coming and took off, hovering above us like a cloud before flying away. Only a few lazy ones remained but we had no food left to give them. And the guard was too close by for us to throw stones.

Then we noticed the train. It was a small train, the length of two lorries. It had been hidden by the shrubs that offered moments of privacy to lovers who frequented the park. Ndaba ran to our parents and came back with some coins. We bought our tickets and rode around the park screaming and shouting at the top of our voices. This was better than Christmas! A few years before it wouldn't have happened. Blacks had not been allowed anywhere near the park. But this was a new Zimbabwe.

The train circled the museum, running past the amphitheatre, the caravan park and campsite, into the jacaranda trees. We found Mother and Father waiting for us, holding hands, smiling and laughing. They were in love. They even kissed. That was the only time I remember my parents kissing. I am not saying they never kissed, just that they never did in front of us.

I have been to the park many times since that picnic. I have been there with friends on Christmas Day, following a tradition. I brought a date once; we sat by the pond, threw in a couple of coins and made a wish to grow old together. When we broke up I remember writing her a poem:

Throw a stone
Make a wish
You whispered
As we danced through the beauty of the park

I threw stones
And coins
And made wishes
Till my hands became too weak
The stones too heavy
And the coins went out of circulation

The people that come to the park now are not lovers with free spirits, they are not families that want a day out, but unemployed people who are hungry and tired of hunting for jobs and are here to rest and hide from prying eyes. They come to the park to plot their next move. The people I see are vagrants who have made the park their home. War veterans have erected a few huts and have been busy pegging small pieces of land to grow crops. The mayor has threatened to forcibly remove them from the park but his threats have remained just that. Threats. The war veterans are untouchable. The country belongs to them.

Today's visit to the park is different. I came here because I wanted to remember that first picnic. I wanted to recreate the same mood. I wanted to see my wife smile and laugh the way my mother had done all those years ago. My wife, Rungano, excuses herself and heads for the toilet as a group of people carrying placards pass through the park headed for the amphitheatre. They are teachers who have been on strike for over three months, plunging the education sector into crisis. Many teachers have left the country for greener pastures.

I look at my daughter, she is just four years old, and wonder what type of education she will get in two years time when she begins school. I want to run around the park and go on a train ride with my daughter. I want to forget about placard carrying teachers. I want to forget about my wife wanting to go to Durban for a holiday when she knows we can't afford it. I want to be happy, to throw my arms around the people that matter to me. My world is different from those demonstrating. At least that is what I think.

My wife comes back from the toilet. "The toilet is locked. It's a public facility for Pete's sake! Now what do I do?" She is angry and I know it is not about the locked toilet. She wants to go to Durban. I have a surprise for her. A big surprise. I don't even know how she will react when I finally tell her.

"You can go behind that tree. No one will see you," I say, almost laughing. She looks at me with murderous eyes but walks behind the tree and squats. No one is looking. She is safe. A group of young teachers pass by. They are toyi-toying and singing revolutionary songs. When I was growing up and going to school teachers used to drive cars. Now they walk.

"I feel cheap, going behind a tree like some rural woman."

"Welcome to Zimbabwe."

"This is not funny. And why are we here in the first place?" Rungana stands close to where I am sitting, as I nibble at a piece of chicken. She is wearing a Faithwear T-shirt and a short white skirt. I love her looks, with her oval face with big brown eyes and thick lips. I wish she was happy just being my wife.

"Mummy, let's go back home. Daddy can stay here if he wants," my daughter says. She has not touched her food. My daughter, with her jeans and her plaited hair, would rather be home watching *Shreck* than be at the park. It's not working. My whole plan is not working. It is as if my wife and daughter are secretly conspiring against me.

"Honey, sit down. We've just arrived. You haven't even touched the food."

"This place is depressing. Look at those teachers. Listen to their songs. Please, let's go somewhere else."

Rungano is an out of work journalist who used to work for the government media, spewing a mixture of lies, propaganda and hate speech. Goebbels style. At first she loved her work, loved seeing her byline hanging on screaming headlines. Gradually it all got to her conscience and she began to hate her job, until one day she lost it and screamed at her editor, telling him she was not a card carrying supporter of the ruling party. She refused to do a story assigned to her and was fired without benefits. Now she occasionally strings for online publications.

"What exactly do you want, Rue?" I ask her.

"You know what I want. You promised to take us to Durban."

She is still standing. Three police cars jam-packed with riot squad drive past, towards the amphitheatre.

"This park business is not for me, maybe ten years ago but not now."

I think of all the trouble I went to in preparing the picnic. I combed the shops looking for rice, chicken and salad cream. There was nothing. Everywhere I went I was greeted by empty shelves and bored, yawning shop assistants who didn't even look up when I walked in and out. I had to get the items from the black market where they cost me an arm and a leg. The food did not cook well. How could it cook well when electricity kept going off and then coming back when the pots had gone cold? Load shedding has become a daily occurrence. I could have bought firewood and cooked outside, but a bundle of firewood now costs more than I can get from the bank as my daily cash allocation. That is if I can manage to sleep in a queue and wait for the banks to open in the morning.

As my anger rises I stand up and walk away. I don't want them to see the anger. My father always told me it is not wise to have two angry people in the same place. I must cool off. The air is hot and the sky is an empty blue that promises nothing more than the heat it is giving in abundance. Suddenly, gunshots shatter the silence of the park. The shots are coming from the direction of the amphitheatre. Before I can open my mouth a wave of people, running and screaming, invade our side of the park. The riot police follow and beat anyone in their way with their batons. The acrid smell of tear gas hits my nose.

"Rue, run!" I scream, running towards my daughter. Rungano looks around in panic. "Run!" I scream again as I grab my daughter and run. Rungano takes too long to react. I see her kick her shoes off, ready to run. The riot police are everywhere. Rungano is swallowed by the running crowd and I lose sight of her for a moment. I run, into the trees, past the broken down train, past the dry pond and onto the main road. The teachers all congregate on the road, blocking traffic. They hesitate to cross into the other half of the park, where the war veterans have come out of their shacks. The police don't follow the teachers onto the road, there seems to be an unwritten agreement as to how far they can pursue them.

"Where is Mummy?" my daughter asks and begins to cry. The tear gas is getting in her eyes.

"She is coming," I say, searching for Rungano in the crowd. The teachers have picked up another song. Their singing is angry, provocative. I see Rungano. She is limping and crying. I run to her.

"They beat me. I didn't do anything but the bastards beat me up."

"Are you hurt?"

"I don't know but my leg and ribs are on fire. Those animals didn't give me a chance to explain."

She wants to sit on the road but I grab her and lead her towards home. It is usually a ten minute walk to the flat but we take longer because of Rungano's limp and the fact that she is not used to walking barefoot.At home Rungano takes off her clothes for me to inspect her injuries. Her skin is a map of brutality. There are bruises on her back and her buttocks have turned purplish. But by now she has stopped crying. I rub herbal ointment into her skin. I can't stop apologizing. I feel responsible for her pain.

"I left my bag at the park. It has my passport and driver's licence in it," she screams at me while I'm rubbing her back with the ointment.

She is still thinking of Durban. I look at her. Then I stand up to go and look for the things left at the park. At the door I decide to tell her about my big surprise. I turn and walk back towards the bed.

"Honey, there is something I need to tell you."

"What is it?" She sits up.

"I left my job."

"You left without discussing it with me first?"

"There was nothing to discuss, Rue."

"So why are you telling me now?"

She falls back onto the bed.

"You know I was not happy. The job was stressful and the salary was peanuts."

"What will you do now? I hope you have a plan."

"I don't. But once I have I will run it by you."

I do have a plan but I don't tell her about it. I turn back and walk out. I know the conversation is not over. When I get to the park it is almost deserted save for the police in riot gear who, in their groups, look like hunting dogs. I walk to where we had stopped for the picnic earlier on. The food lies scattered. I find one of Rungano's shoes. The handbag is gone, but the passport and driver's licence are placed neatly on a concrete bench. Thoughtful. I wonder whether it was the police or someone else. A teacher perhaps. I look around for the other shoe. It is nowhere to be found.

The park has surely changed. It is no longer friendly. The lawn is gone. The green is gone. The water and the rainbows are gone. The pond is drier than the Kalahari desert. The fish are gone, replaced by rotting used condoms. The birds are all gone. Even the guards are gone. In their place I see mean looking riot police. Only the train remains but it is in no shape to move or carry anyone.

Four riot police advance towards me. I start walking away. "You, stop right there!" one of them barks.

I put the passport and licence in my trouser pocket and wait for them. Mistake number one.

"Teacher, what are you still doing here? We gave an order for everyone to disperse a long time ago." They are breathing in my face.

"I'm not a teacher." All four of them are staring at me, brandishing black batons. Their eyes are red as if they have been smoking *mbanje*.

"I'm not a teacher," I repeat.

"Then prove to us that you are not a teacher."

Instinctively my hand goes towards my wallet and then I remember that when I left my job I handed over my professional identity card. Mistake number two.

"I'm sorry, but-" They don't wait for me to finish the sentence. Four batons rain on my flesh. The blows come from all directions and land everywhere. Head. Back. Hands. Stomach. Everywhere. I howl in pain. Realizing that if I didn't do anything they could kill me, I hurl myself at one of them. I take him by surprise. He hits the ground with a thud. In anger I kick him between the legs before I run off with the three other police officers close on my heels. I am bleeding from the nose and mouth. A tooth is missing. My left arm and ribs feel broken.

When I get home Rungano screams. "What happened to you?"

"The riot police thought I was one of the teachers."

My daughter sees me and starts to cry. Tears cloud Rungano's eyes. I can't let them see me cry. Not now. I have a plan. My mind is made up. We will leave Zimbabwe. We will go to Durban after all.

Crossroads

Novuyo Rosa Tshuma

19.23

There are shadows that lurk within the shadows at the border. Shadows that embrace the dark corners and watch those in the light. Some shadows make themselves known. They walk up and down like patrolmen, their eyes openly searching those in the queue, defiant, rude. As they skulk past, limbs involuntarily wrap themselves around bodies and handbags are clutched ever more tightly in the pits of arms. Cowardly shadows, that look for cowardly opportunities. A stray in desperate need of the toilet. A careless teenager in the throngs of lustful conversation on an expensive little flip up.

I move closer to Tari.

"It's the same when you're going back home, but in reverse," Tari tells me. "You go through the South African side with no problem, but when you get to the Zim side, *hokoyo*, five, six, seven, eight hours of waiting."

"You've been here before?"

"My dear, I pass through here every two to three weeks. Two weeks in South Africa, two weeks in Zimbabwe." He leans forward, covers his mouth with his palm. "I'm into buying and selling, I do everything and anything. It used to be petrol, even rands for forex. That is until those bastards top-up-there made forex legal tender."

He leans back and laughs. A loud, rehearsed laugh, like he's said this many times before, determined to squeeze in the laugh at this precise moment. I smile politely. People are staring at us.

Tari is a friend I picked up on the bus, a friend I will drop when we get to Park Station in Johannesburg. Somebody to show me the ropes at the border. Company along the way, as I battle to sleep while the stereo just above my head blasts a nuisance of lively guitars in my ear. Simon Chimbetu, Tari explains.

I nod.

Chopa Chimbetu and the Dandara Express.

I nod.

He attended their show just the week before, at the Harare Gardens. Massive, he adds. Did I know how to dance *nsungura*?

I yawn.

You do not count the hours when you are standing in a queue that outruns the distance of your eye. You shuffle along mechanically, stare into oblivion. Look up at the night sky and search the stars for patterns. A rose, complete with a stem. The wing of a bird.

"T for Tari," he says, pointing at an obscure shape.

"Hmm."

When you're tired of looking up, you watch those around you. The couple in front of you that seem impossibly young. The boy looks sixteen. The girl looks much younger, perhaps because of her small body. Her stomach sticks out in front of her like an anomaly, her back bent to accommodate the weight. Her scrawny limbs grow out of her form like they were stuck there as an afterthought. She looks such a child, barrelling not a pregnancy but kwashiorkor in one of those 'give aid to Africa' advertisements. She continuously rubs the arm of her boyfriend, leans over to whisper something in his ear, leans back to laugh at something he has said. He indulges her, like a decoration on display at a party.

When you've run out of things to do and look at, and your new-found friend is lost in his own thoughts, you shut down into semi-sleep. Your arms are folded across your chest, your eyes are focused on some point in the distance, and you are trying not to think. It's a skill we've all learned in the game of waiting. Which is why, even in this godforsaken queue, even as people sigh and shuffle their feet and say,

"*Hayi ah*."

"I thought I had left this back home."

"*Shuwa*."

they are still cheerful, filled with the heat of the night and laughter and all sorts of tales about Johannesburg.

"My cell phone was stolen the first day I arrived. They asked for it and I gave it to them. *Phela*, I'm told you never fight when they ask for your phone. You can be stabbed and die, all for a phone."

"You're lucky they asked for it. *Mina bangifaka amampamampama*, they gave me a good slap or two before asking for my phone. I never carry an expensive phone, I have one of those cheap hundred rand Nokia ones. So when they saw it, they slapped me again for having such a useless phone, and smashed it on the ground."

"You're lucky all you got was a slap. They had a knife in my face. I couldn't go anywhere by myself for weeks."

"You're lucky all they did was hold the knife to your face. They stabbed me. I would show you but the scar is on my bum."

They are never-ending, these tales about the great big bustling City of Gold. They become more imaginative by the minute.

The pregnant girl who looks like she's suffering from kwashiorkor is pleading with the immigration officer. Her boyfriend stands rigid by her side, watching helplessly.

"No," the immigration woman says. "How can I let you pass when it says you only have one more day? Denied."

She picks up a stamp.

"Please, please," the girl entreats, bending her knees and cupping her hands like a beggar. "Last time I got my days at the Home Affairs Office-"

"Denied," the immigration woman repeats, banging the stamp on her passport. "Go back. Next!"

"Eish, please I'm begging you-"

"Next!"

I shuffle forward, slip my passport through the opening in the glass partition. The pregnant girl is holding her passport in dismay, staring at it like her world has just shattered into a million irretrievable pieces. DENIED runs diagonally across the page. Her boyfriend puts a stiff arm around her. Hope knows no bounds. To come all this way, on a nearly expired visa.

I hear a man say to the pregnant girl, "You went about it the wrong way. How can you expect to change her mind when you are pleading so publicly? Are you trying to make a fool out of her?" He looks around conspiratorially. "You need to talk to someone, one on one...." He rubs his thumb against his fingers. "Grease a few palms."

He walks away, leaving the tear-stricken girl and her boyfriend staring after him with dumbfounded expressions.

As I walk away, head for the bus, I smother my passport in soggy, popping kisses. Once you get through that immigration building, once you get through, it's as if you could fly. Those hours in the queue have evaporated; the pain of it is to be savoured.

It is indeed a long way to the border, much much longer than the road distance. It is a distance measured not in kilometres, but in sweat and tears and ingenuity, beguiling smiles and the tallest of lies. Begging, begging, and more begging.

You have to rise before the sun. If it is on a day when there is no electricity, you may have to fumble in the dark. You will wake your relatives or not wake your relatives, depending on who you have come to stay with, in the capital city Harare, where all the embassies are situated. If it is where you are not welcome, where it is only necessity that has brought you, and the begrudging ties of blood that have welcomed you, you will not wake anyone to ask for a candle, but make do with the dark. Sometimes there is no water, depending on where you are staying. And so you may find yourself having to wet your towel and wipe the sleep from your body. A quick, rigorous exercise; face, armpits, between your legs.

Again, there may be no food. Or it may be there, but you may not feel comfortable touching it without permission. And so you may find yourself stepping out into a morning where the darkness is just beginning to recede, burdened by a grumbling stomach. There is no time for fear, no time to even think of it. You have summoned the Higher Powers to walk with you, and so nothing of this semi-darkness will touch you.

You catch a *kombi*, or two *kombis*, to the South African Embassy, depending on where you have been staying. The South African Embassy is in an area awash with embassies, a discreet, quiet neighbourhood with wide roads and houses with big yards. *Diplomatic*. You see the signs pointing out directions to the different embassies as you walk down the road from where you dropped off. The British Embassy. The American Embassy. The Embassy of Kuwait – that one must be a very lonely one, who goes to Kuwait? When you finally reach the South African Embassy, you are dismayed to discover that, for all your efforts, the queue already runs the perimeter fence and peters out into the road. It is the only embassy that is bustling with activity at this early hour.

Hawkers march up and down with their wares, pens and cigarettes, *freezits* and cool drinks, bananas and *mabhanzi*. There is even a photographer, who points at a makeshift studio under a tree and yells, "Passport size photos, visa photos, any photo that they want I take, cheap cheap photos *varumwe*, good quality photos, photos photos...."

He looks in the eye of every one he passes, as though he is able to will them into needing his services.

The most amazing type of hawker approaches you the moment you join the tail of the queue.

"Sista, it is obvious from your place in the line, that you will not make it. They only take fifty people a day." A dramatic pause. "But I can help you sista, my place is number twenty three. I will happily sell it to you."

You stare at the woman, as those within hearing distance turn to stare at you. She is a short woman wearing a white, dirty *doek* and a matching, shapeless skirt that drops all the way to her toes. She regards you with a serious expression, wearing that air of business.

You eye her suspiciously. "How much?"

"Only a hundred rand."

You shake your head. A hundred is too much.

"How much do you have, sista?"

You shake your head and turn away.

"Come, *vasikana*, we can talk. How much do you have? How about fifty?"

You shake your head. She shrugs and walks away. "Obvious you don't want a visa, sista."

"They are crooks, these people," somebody says. "Coming here to make the queue unnecessarily long for those of us who mean business. One day, they will get what's coming to them."

"We should complain to the Embassy."

"Heh, complain? Once you get in there, do you think you have time to complain about such things? It's hard enough to get a visa, please."

"We should deal with them ourselves. Do you know some of them sleep here? The whole night, like *varoyi*."

Another ingenious method of making a living. Sleeping outside the embassy, queuing for those who do not have the means to be here early, charging a fee for 'services rendered'. There is nothing that one cannot do here anymore. One's ability to make money is limited only by the scope of one's creativity.

The sun sails over the rooftops, a warm morning that quickly progresses into a sweltering heat. The loose lilac blouse clings to your back. You watch as the embassy cars arrive, one by one, Pajeros and Range Rovers and Mercedes, driving through the embassy gates. The occupants step out, remove their sunglasses only to greet each other, before putting them back on and strolling towards the buildings. Waiting. Waiting. More waiting. There is nothing special about it; it is everywhere. Your generation may wait all their lives. In the end, people will forget what it is they are waiting for.

The queue begins to move at a very efficient pace, and people begin to come alive. Hope has raised its head. Alas! It has awakened too early. You aren't even halfway down the perimeter fence when you hear that they have taken enough people for the day. You will come again tomorrow, to find a long queue in which you know you will not make it. But hope has no bounds. We wait and wait, in hopeless queues, like the trained dogs we've become.

The following day. You look for the woman with the *doek*. She's still in the same *doek* and the same skirt, and the same shiny blue blouse. You sniff the air, searching for the stench of her body, and when you find it, you snatch your head back, as though her stench comes as a surprise.

"I have forty," you say to her.

"Ah sista, at least put another ten rand on top."

"Forty is all I have. Take it or leave it."

"*Horayiti*, take it easy, sista. Today you are very lucky, I am number *sixisteeni*."

Inside the embassy compound, you are given numbers, and made to stand in a queue that moves at a snail's pace. The sun is unrelenting. The heat is vicious. The air collapses under a hundred different body smells. A large woman comes out once in a while to call out the numbers. People seem to take forever in there. You watch the time until you no longer watch the time. Finally, your number is called. You snap up your slouching body, hurry forward.

When it is your turn at the counter, you swallow hard. You have heard the most horrific stories about these people, how they will find practically any excuse to turn you away. You pray that you have one of the good ones. Everyone behind the counter is a woman. You wish they did not use women. Now there is no advantage you can wield over them, no eyelashes you can bat, no hips you can sway. The woman does not even look up as she ruffles through your papers. You have all the necessary documents, double checked and triple checked before you came. Police Clearance. Seduced out of an officer old enough to be your father. A phone number had to be proffered, fake promises of a get-together made. You intend to be long gone by then. Two thousand rands worth of travellers' cheques. Money borrowed from Mi, your aunt who lives in South Africa, which you must give back upon arrival. A valid passport. Palms greased for this one. Corruption grins at every stage of the hierarchy. The woman does not look up as she directs you to yet another queue to pay an administration fee, tells you to come for your visa in two weeks' time.

Triumph. It is a bitter-sweet, fleeting emotion.

The photographer is calling out to you for a photo even as you leave the embassy.

00.06

Somebody has a wicked sense of humour. There is a poster in the cubicles of the public toilets on the South African side of the border that reads:

TOILET PAPER ONLY
TO BE USED IN THIS TOILET
NO CARDBOARD
NO CLOTH
NO ZIM DOLLARS
NO NEWSPAPER

I take a picture. A keepsake, to show my children one day, when my country is no longer lying on its back with its legs spread apart, in an act of incest with its fathers and their children. Pain is sweet only in retrospect. Humiliation only funny as an afterthought.

The bus chugs away from the border. There is that feeling of exhilaration upon sight of the sign 'Musina'. We make a stop by the first service station we come across.

"Ten minutes!" bellows the driver.

Even the lights here seem brighter, more cheerful. It's amazing the things that will make one leap with joy. No more power cuts. No more water shortages. No more queues. Joy is an emotion that never matures. I buy in a frenzy. A packet of Simba chips, Cadbury chocolate, a can of coke, bottled water, a chicken and mushroom pie. A packet of pinky sweets. Haven't had those since I was a child. I feel like such a kid.

Tari is ever chatty, playing the tourist guide.

"Pretoria and Johannesburg spill into one another. There is no bush area separating them. You will see, when you get there. And the urban landscape glittering with lights is absolutely beautiful at night. You'll see."

I cannot wait to see.

Triumph.

The promise of auspicious beginnings.

05.07

Johannesburg, bathed in the first light of the morning. The sun is stirring from her slumber. Being in this place feels like being in a different space altogether Geography has been reshaped by metropolitan structures. The land is familiar in terms of climate and structure. Beyond that, the familiar is made peculiar by foreign forms.

You cannot tell when you have left Pretoria and entered Jo'burg, unless you read the signs on the sides of the road. Big signs. How can you get lost in this place? The two cities, as Tari said, spill into one another. No space is left to waste.

Johannesburg. A labyrinth of winding, wide highways that crisscross each other, elevated on an architecture of firm concrete. As you approach the city centre, buildings emerge from green landscapes, factories and hotels and office buildings protruding as though they have always been there, since the beginning of time.

"Imagine! This could have been us," Tari breathes. He sighs a sad sigh.

Johannesburg. A city centre of high rises, concrete and steel, brick and mortar, tarmac and paint. Signs and posters and more signs and posters. Cheerful creativity is splashed on billboards. The stiletto of a woman next to a steaming cup of coffee. *Well, would you?* running across the bottom. Well, would you what? The motivators of liberal thought. *Think outside the box,* says another billboard, with the words swimming in a background of nothingness. Where I come from, we've learned to think without the box.

A fresh wind blows in the early morning. Cars dot the highway. It is 05.13.

Park Station is deceptively calm at this hour, a current gathering momentum before the chaos. Our old bus rumbles into the bay, belches and farts, *Ntswiiiii.*

Tari offers his hand. "It was good to meet you."

I smile. "Me too."

"Can I have your number?"

"Well, I've only just arrived so…."

"Can I give you mine?"

70

"Ok."

He hands me a piece of paper with the scribblings of his name and two phone numbers, adds his email address as an afterthought.

"You on Facebook?" he asks.

I shake my head.

"You ought to join Facebook. Then look for me, and send me a friend request. OK?"

"OK."

"Great. Well, good luck, and hope to see you soon!"

He turns to leave and I wave goodbye.

09.16

Mi lives in a room. A room in a series of rooms full of god-knows-how-many people, rooms that together make a narrow, rickety building that rushes towards a phantom salvation in the sky.

Shock. It renders pretence possible. Pretence. A useless art among people who look beyond what they see. Mi searches my face as we walk in, her eyes dancing in their sockets like they are doing a jive to a fast number. She must find what she is looking for, in my face, what I am trying so desperately to hide behind a plastic smile and a "Ah, what a nice little place!"

Words I regret the moment they slip out. They reek of insincerity. They spit an unintended sarcasm. Mi curls her lower lip, looks away, points to the corner, where I am to place my bags. She leans against the wall, lowers herself to the floor. She fumbles for a cigarette. Steadies it between her lips, while she flicks the lighter and brings the flame to the tip. Inhales, holds the smoke, blows it through her nose. Sighs.

In a Park Station that had suddenly erupted to life with the morning, a laughing Mi hugged me, pulled back, hugged me some more.

"Hmm, you're so thin!" she exclaimed.

"Good to see you too, Mi," I grinned.

She picked up one of my bags. Said, with a curtsy and a wide sweep of the arm, "Welcome to Jozi *neh*."

I spoke in Ndebele. She responded in Ndebele-Zulu peppered with a Zulu accent, punctuated by *neh, neh! neh?* I wanted to say, "Hey! It's me! You don't have to pretend, it's all right." But I sensed the gulf that was suddenly between us. A place can change a person. But that is what we came here for, isn't it? To find ourselves anew.

She was chatty as we left the station, stepped out into a world that jolts you, upon first glance. The noise of chatter is everywhere. Voices lambast you from all angles, fighting with the angry 'beep beep' of the *kombis* to be heard. The screech of squealing tyres. The screaming stench of human form. Stalls have been set up on the pavements, leaving a narrow strip on which the dense crowds must negotiate. But the pavement is not enough; the stalls spill out onto the road, rickety erections that slant at odd angles, leaning against one another like a row of jolly, intoxicated gentlemen struggling to appear sober in front of a lady. A gamut of goods are on display. Leather belts and padlocks, clothing and satchels, mosquito coils and an assortment of perfumes. A phone shop. Meat sizzling on a *braai* stand. A piece falls off the stand onto the ground. The proprietor picks it up, throws it back onto the fire.

The noise is of people. The stench is of people. A colourful reverberation of human life.

Man is a chameleon.

"The first thing you need to do," Mi said as we took sail in this human sea, "is to get a job. There are a couple of people I know who can help you."

I nodded. "Yes, and after a year or so, I will have saved up enough money for university."

She did not say anything.

"Wow," I said, looking around me. "This place is big!"

"You haven't even seen the half of it."

You will not see the dirt and the grime and how some of these buildings squat uncomfortably amidst the filth. Not on your first day. Not when you still look at this mirage of a utopia with hope-filled eyes. Not yet.

Poverty will start to lose its glamour when you reach the building of many rooms. It is not a naked poverty, mind you. It is not a poverty of a war of guns and machetes. Not a poverty of Sudan women laden with bags of baby bones balloonin' with bloated bellies. Not a poverty of never-ending queues, or empty supermarkets. This is a poverty that shines, that is still able to smile in its quest for wealth. A poverty that proclaims that the gold is out there, and it is going to find it. This poverty makes you giddy with the cheap hope it peddles.

So here we are. In Mi's room. There is a mattress on the floor. A two-plate stove by the corner. A freezer next to it. Clothes spilling out of a Tshangane bag. Skirts, a bra, thongs. A man's shirt. An iron sits next to the pile. A poster of Michael Jackson in his classical pose, clutching his crotch, hangs behind the door.

"Things have been hard," Mi says, letting the smoke out through her nose. "Things around here are *hard*. It's hard if you don't have any papers and you don't have any money. All that crap about things being easy here that you hear back home, forget it."

I stare. I do not know what to say. These things she's saying, I don't want to hear them. They depress me. This is not what I came here for.

"School and all that crap, my dear, forget it. I came here, as naïve as you are, with nothing but a pocketful of dreams. But look at me."

That's you, I want to say. *It's not gonna be me.*

I smile, because she's staring at me and I suppose she expects some sort of reaction. I am smiling and suddenly I resent her for the things she's saying. I clutch the piece of paper with Tari's contact details, scrunched up in my sweaty palm. I will leave this dump as soon as I can. I am feeling uncomfortable because Mi's gaze does not waver and I'm beginning to think that perhaps she can discern what it is I'm thinking.

I keep smiling.

She keeps staring.

The Piano Tuner

Bryony Rheam

Leonard Mwale climbed slowly and heavily down the steps of the minibus, holding the door frame with one hand and beginning to fumble in his trouser pocket with his other. He could feel the impatience of the driver as he pumped the accelerator a little. The conductor waved at him slowly, as though he were a child and flashed him a big, cheesy, open-mouthed grin, before looking down at the wad of notes in his hand.

Once out, Leonard wiped his brow with a large white handkerchief and stepped away as the minibus roared off. He let the bag he was carrying on his right shoulder slip to the ground softly. His top lip glistened with sweat as he pushed two fingers into his waistcoat pocket and pulled out a small piece of paper.

He hadn't been to this area of Ndola for a long time. Most of the pianos he tuned these days were at schools, but there were still a few in private households. Sometimes the ladies came to fetch him, or sent a driver. If not, they usually paid his bus fare and gave him lunch. But this madame hadn't mentioned anything of the kind and he was still too polite to mention it. He'd simply written her address down and said that he would be there at ten. He would have to walk quickly if he was going to make it on time. Being October, it was already hot and the tar shimmered before him as he picked up his bag and started down the road.

He was a heavily built man who walked slowly, almost painfully, yet there was rarely a sense of weariness about his person. He always wore a suit, a three-piece in brown. It was a habit he had picked up from Tom Jenkins, the man who had taught him how to tune pianos all those years ago in Lusaka – 46 to be exact. He remained fervent about it, even when he heard titters of laughter as he toiled along the road, sweating in the African sun, and even when nice madames offered him long, cool glasses of water and suggested he take his jacket off.

When he had almost reached the address of his next job, he stopped for a moment, put down his bag and mopped his head again with his handkerchief. He took his watch out of a pocket and checked the time. He was a minute early. The large green metal gate was closed to him so he pushed the button on the intercom and waited, trying to calm his breathing so he could speak clearly. He needn't have worried for the gate opened and he walked in, up a straight driveway, lined with rows of meticulously trimmed shrubs. To his left was a small patch of equally well-kept grass that didn't look as though it had a blade out of place. On a small verandah were two pots sporting large ferns, and a stack of wrought iron chairs, chained together with a padlock securing them.

A gardener appeared in the empty garage at the end of the driveway and called something, which Leonard didn't hear, and pointed in the direction of the back door. Leonard opted for the front door, pausing once again to mop his brow before he knocked. A maid appeared almost immediately and Leonard heard the sound of various locks being turned before the door was opened. Despite the heat, the maid looked wonderfully cool in her uniform of dress, apron and *doek*. She had a bright, open face and smiled widely at Leonard, who warmed to her at once.

"Good morning," he greeted her. "I am here to tune the piano. Please tell the madame."

"I know. Follow me," and she stood back so that he could enter. The house, of the old, colonial type, was dark and cool inside. He followed the maid through an inside verandah and along a short passage. She opened a door on the right and ushered him in. It was a sparsely furnished room: a small round table in the middle covered in a white crocheted tablecloth and an upright piano against the far wall. Leonard stood at the door for a couple of seconds, as though awaiting instructions.

"The madame... she is here?" he ventured.

"She will come," said the maid, but there was something in her voice that suggested it wasn't likely. Leonard approached the piano, put down his bag and pulled out the stool. He turned just as the maid was pulling the door behind her.

"Sister," he called and she stopped. "Some water please. Cold."

There was that smile again and she closed the door. Leonard turned to the piano and pushed back the lid. When the maid entered some minutes later with a jug of water and a plastic tumbler, Leonard was lost in his work and oblivious to her presence.

When he stopped and poured himself some water, he sat and listened for a few minutes, but he could hear nothing. Then somewhere, far in the distance, he heard a voice calling to someone, probably the gardener shouting to a friend. Otherwise, there was nothing: no television or radio, no sound of voices from within the house, no tread of feet down the passage.

Towards lunchtime, there was a light knock at the door and the maid entered.

"The Bwana is asking if you would like to be having lunch with them."

Leonard hesitated. It wasn't that he didn't want to accept the invitation; just that he had hoped to get in another job that afternoon.

"Yes, thank you. Tell the Bwana thank you, I will come."

"This way," said the maid and pointed back down the corridor they had walked up earlier. Her response took him by surprise and it was only then that he realised he had received an order, not an invitation. He held up his hand for her to wait while he put a few things away, then he pushed the piano stool back into place and followed her.

The maid knocked on one side of a large double door with glass inlay. Leonard heard a sharp "Come in!" and she pushed the handle down and opened the door for him, without going into the room herself.

A large Indian man sat at the head of the far end of the table, knife and fork in hands, his plate piled high with food. He was in his fifties with thinning black hair and a bulbous face. His shirt collar was open to reveal a thick tuft of hair and a thin line of perspiration was making its way down his face. Next to him sat a tall thin lady with a long gaunt face. Her hair was pulled back into a loose knot high on her head. She played with the food on her half-empty plate with desultory interest. The man looked briefly at Leonard and then took a mouthful of food.

"Yes?" he said, when he had finished swallowing and had wiped his hands on a serviette.

"Leonard Mwale, sir," said Leonard, extending his hand and walking over to him.

The name obviously didn't register with the man who merely looked at Leonard's hand without taking it.

"The piano tuner," prompted Leonard with a brief laugh.

"Ah," said the man. "And where is the Bwana?"

"The Bwana? I am the Bwana, sir. I work by myself."

"But it says here 'Thomas Jenkins, Piano Tuners'" said the man, picking up a business card at his elbow. "This isn't your name. This is a *mzungu* name. Where is the *mzungu*?"

Leonard laughed; a deep, hearty, good-natured laugh. "Ah, Bwana Jenkins left this country a long time ago. I have his business now. I am the piano tuner."

The man didn't share Leonard's sense of humour. "Mmm," he muttered uncertainly, turning the card over in his hand. "The *mzungu* bwana let you take his business, huh? What, you didn't buy it from him?"

Leonard stopped laughing. There was an accusatory note in the man's voice. He spoke quietly but defiantly, "He gave it to me. A long time ago now, in 1965. He was leaving the country to go back to England and he gave me his business so that there would still be someone in Zambia who could tune pianos."

"Hmmm? There is no one else?"

Leonard shook his head. "Sometimes someone comes from South Africa or Zimbabwe. But they are expensive, very expensive."

The man appeared to think this over. "You are good?" he said, finally. "You are as good as these people from South Africa and Zimbabwe?"

Leonard lowered his head, a little embarrassed.

"Yes, sir, I am as good as them." Then he added with a return of his laugh, "But half the price."

The man stared at him for a few more seconds before turning to the woman and speaking to her in a language Leonard did not understand. Finally he looked up and pointed his hand to the chair at the other end of the table opposite himself. The maid was called and she moved the mat and cutlery from the right hand side of the man and set a place for Leonard. While placing a glass next to him, the man called something out to her and she disappeared, returning shortly with the plastic tumbler she had brought in to Leonard earlier.

"I have to go to work," said the man, standing up and pushing his chair back. "Paying for your piano lessons is keeping me busy at the office," he said to the tall, thin lady. "You are going to work me into an early grave."

She didn't say a word, sipping her water quietly and staring ahead. The man nodded at Leonard and then left. Shortly afterwards, the lady left the room without saying anything.

The job took longer than Leonard thought it would and he still wasn't happy with an 'A' flat which sounded too dull for his liking. He sat playing for a few minutes. There was some music on top of the piano that he glanced through and chose a light piece by Beethoven.

"You play beautifully," said a voice from the door. Leonard turned and there was the lady from lunch. He stood and gestured for her to sit down.

"Come, play. See how it sounds now."

She shook her head.

"I can't... I couldn't... I can't play like you just did. I'm just a beginner. I've only just got the piano."

Leonard smiled and sat down again. He carried on playing, finishing with an exaggerated flourish. The woman edged nearer, leaning against the table, her arms crossed over her chest.

"Very nice, very nice," she kept saying. "Ah, I wish I could play like you."

"Lessons," said Leonard, simply. "You are taking lessons?"

"Do you give them?" she asked with sudden excitement. "I will pay you very well. Double."

Leonard laughed. "No, no, I do not give lessons. I am the piano tuner."

Leonard accepted payment for the piano tuning, counting it out meticulously. Then he smiled and gave the woman a receipt. She looked at it, reading the name on the stamp.

"Thomas Jenkins, Piano Tuners," she said and then burst into laughter. "Thank you, Mr Jenkins!"

Leonard gave her a big, generous smile. He felt sorry for her, as though she were lost, but no one was able to give her directions home.

"Thank you," he said. "Give me a call in about six months' time."

Her face fell. "So soon? My husband...."

"It's the weather, you know. After the rainy season, it might not sound the same."

"Okay," she agreed, uncertainly.

"And I give discounts for good customers," he smiled. "Good afternoon." He turned and made his way towards the door. She started after him.

"Mr Mwale," she called. "My driver can take you home. Let me call him."

"Thank you," said Leonard. "That would be kind of you."

Later, when he had been dropped at home and had poured himself a glass of water, Leonard removed his jacket and took the money the lady had given him from his pocket. He had not told her it was short. He knew where the money had come from and he understood.

The Poetry Slammer

Nyevero Muza

Nhamo is what you might call a closet writer. He secretly struggles with the balancing act of holding a full time job to put food on the table and finding enough time to write. In his late teens, he was quite optimistic about his literary prospects, declaring confidently that he would publish his first novel by the age of twenty. Now his rose-tinted glasses have acquired a patina of despondency and the hue of unfulfilled ambition clouds his vision.

With the benefit of hindsight, he realises that it was this misguided but well-meaning ambition to be a published writer that distracted him from his 'A' Level studies and prevented him from proceeding to university, by which selfish act he denied his clan the prestige of its first university graduate.

Sometimes, he rationalises that it all worked out for the best because – ironically – by that very act of failure, he rescued himself from a career in engineering into whose arms the twin evils of peer pressure and purely materialistic ends were ushering him. Those days you had to study sciences at 'A' Level, preferably the magical combination of MPC (Maths, Physics and Chemistry) and then aspire to become an electrical engineer or any other kind of engineer if you entertained any thought of being considered 'cool'. He is convinced that, if he had yielded to such a temptation, any artistic impulses within him would have curled up and become what he soon might be – artistic biltong. After many years of holding a nine-to-five job, his soul has finally been signed, sealed and delivered to the rat race – but Nhamo refuses to completely bury his literary ambitions. He writes whenever he can, which is not often, but still reads a lot for a man so immersed in the staid world of banking.

He admires those who seem to be comfortable in their artistic skins, effortlessly managing to have their voices heard. Those like **X**, the gritty character in his new short story, who can raise their voice above the din of mediocrity. He is convinced that this is the story that will make people sit up and take notice. And so, for the umpteenth time, he sits at the expansive desk in his study to read it again....

X was a poetry slammer who haunted The Café. **X** was his *nom de guerre* and it had become his only means of identification. The name set him apart from the crowd and he liked its association with voting, its symbolism of the right to choose. The name originated from the chopping, axe-like movements he made with his hands to accompany his razor-sharp wit when he recited poetry. They used to call him Axe but, over time, he dropped first the 'e' and then the 'A', initially to banish any violent connotations and ultimately to embrace the full symbolism of **X**. He insisted that the **X** must be written as a bold capital because that is what he was – bold. He became so attached to this name that after some time, he composed a short poem in honour of it. Despite the protestations of his colleagues that this was an exercise in vanity, he used it to introduce himself to his audiences:

> Whether it's the ballot
> Or the bullet,
> **X** marks the vote,
> **X** marks the spot.

X and his kindred spirits met at The Café, home to the lyrical guerrillas who prowled the urban jungle, once a month – sometimes twice – to strut their stuff and provide entertainment and escape for one and all. He was the one who, during his three minutes of fame, gesticulated rhythmically to seen and unseen audiences; his eyes slammed shut as he chanted strings of words that went straight for the jugular. The silent music he heard and danced to was difficult to define – sometimes slow and soulful when his lean body swayed with an easy grace and sometimes fast and furious when he shook and convulsed, his voice loud and guttural.

They all seemed to wear dreadlocks, these slammers, as if they were some kind of badge of honour signifying a rite of passage into the charmed world of wordsmiths where exotic words like alliteration, consonance and assonance were glibly dropped. For **X**, the locks were not just *hair*; they were a performance tool; accentuating his head movements and contrasting sharply with the blood red backdrop that shouted – POETRY SLAM!

Those who saw him perform will tell you that, in full flight, **X** was a spider, spinning webs that trapped the audience. His words struck fear into the heart of the matter. At the poetry slams, anyone could spin any yarn, shoot from the hip or speak off the cuff. It didn't matter how because there was freedom *of* expression; as for freedom *after* expression; well that was – and still is – another matter.

Anything could be on the agenda, but for **X** it was usually about 'The Struggle' that had been hijacked and betrayed by what he called 'armchair revolutionaries'. So when he recited a poem like *A Struggle for Hire*, the audience went into thraldom and joined him, catching his heat in spontaneous combustion, amid frenzied shouts of Ahoy! Ahoy! Ahoy!

This struggle is a muddle
It does nothing but fumble
Infiltrated and annihilated
Privatised and commodified
Oh, it's a trivial, commercial pursuit

This struggle has lost its sparkle
Once a rumble in the jungle
It's now petrified and pacified
Denatured and domesticated
Resistance in this instance
No longer a nuisance to malfeasance

This struggle is at a standstill
It's grist for greed's mill
This struggle is for hire
It needs some fire, not just any fire
But *more* fire!

The enthusiasm of the poet and his audience told of those who had travelled this road before, feeding off each other's energy every step of the way. Most of the time, he recited his own poems but sometimes he recited those of others, *Still I Rise* by Maya Angelou and *A Dream Deferred* by Langston Hughes being his favourites. **X** said that he did not wish to be a martyr, but if having his say made him one, then so be it. That, he said, is the essence of poetry. Sacrifice.

Another thing he felt strongly about was that "poetry is not a non-aligned movement, so it does not sit on fences or cruise the highways of sentimentality. Real poetry must be in the trenches getting its hands dirty." That is why his own poetry was out on the streets brawling with complacency prejudice and ignorance. Ruffling feathers and asking questions. For dramatic effect, he swore that if you met a street kid who pressed his snotty nose against your car window and asked for money to buy food, that was probably one of his poems. It was partly because of this conviction about the importance of poetry for human survival and partly due to his love for surfing the internet that he discovered Audre Lorde's article *Poetry Is Not A Luxury*. From then on, he never missed the opportunity to tell you about "poetry as illumination, for it is through poetry that we give names to those ideas which are – until the poem – nameless and formless, about to be birthed, but already felt...."

At only 22, **X** had become something of a celebrity at The Café. He was easy to love, if not for the unquestionable devotion to his craft, then for the sometimes awkward charm with which he pursued it. Everyone agreed that if he kept his shoulder to the wheel, he would 'become someone' or make it to the European poetry grand slams with exotic names such as *Grand Slam de Poésie*.

The only regret **X** had is that, unlike some of the other poets, he neither wrote nor performed poetry in his mother tongue. When, during one of the frequent debates at The Café, some well-read person, quoting T.S. Elliot, remarked that a poet's responsibility is first and foremost to his or her language, he switched to his first language for a while, but the lack of a vital spark in his poetry was there for all to see. Even as he beat a hasty retreat to the relative comfort of the English language, **X**'s consolation was that there was no shortage of fellow poets who had something to say in the vernacular and – given the opportunity – said it well, sometimes even better than him.

X was what they called a 'Born Free', born after independence in 1980, so he never experienced the war of liberation. He infuriated his father when he said that he couldn't understand why there was still a big hoo-ha about a conflict that ended three decades ago.

"This maddening *Chimurenga* that preoccupies your mind and refuses to go away; why," he once asked his father, "do you cling to it so tenaciously if it brings back such painful memories?"

"Forgiving is easy son, forgetting is not," was his father's response to what he considered this frivolous and vexatious question.

X acknowledged that the struggle had been long and hard, but he swore that he now faced a much more debilitating one just to survive from one day to the next in a free Zimbabwe. His parents'pictures from the 60s and 70s oozed a glamorous charm, a sure-footedness absent from their present circumstances. Sometimes, in unguarded moments, his father admitted that he missed the good old days 'when money was money' and 'friends were friends'.

"Father, what you experienced during that time was real and formidable, but the more *your* generation insists that *my* generation pay homage to those painful experiences, the more irrelevant they seem to the present day," X once said.

"Son, it is the duty of *my* generation to ensure that *your* generation does not take for granted the freedom and dignity that we enjoy today. They were made possible by the hardship and suffering of many people, some of whom lost their lives in the process," his father responded in a polite but firm tone.

Aware of the direction in which the discussion might steer itself, X moved to put the matter to rest.

"I know, Father, because you say it all the time. I know not only because the history books say so, but also because it is true. But much as I would like to *feel* what you *felt,* and *see* what you *saw*, I could never have your ears nor your eyes. You have to accept that what was of great concern in the past might have become of less concern now. Every generation must fight its own demons." His tone conveyed finality.

Like most of his old comrades, X's father was a policeman. Behind his back, X called him *Ngonjo* or, to his face, 'War Vet'. Every month, X's father waged fierce battles with inflation just to put food on the table and pay bills for services that no one bothered to deliver any more. These stresses often led to battles between his parents, which enveloped X's father with a loud sort of silence that clung to him like a brewing storm. That was when he stormed out of the house and disappeared to the 'other woman'. Battered and bruised, X's mother was determined to carry on with the necessary business of existence because 'it's the nature of men to stray, and the nature of men to come back, even if on their deathbed.' He would be gone for days, this father of his, who had the temper of a loaded gun in a terrorist's hands, but when he returned he would be almost unrecognisable – ever so apologetic and even regretful. The 'other woman' was a policewoman whose husband had not returned from the war in the DRC. X's mother stoically refused to acknowledge this 'small house', preferring instead to vent her frustration by waging an endless struggle with the municipal police, who were determined to prevent her and the other women of the township from selling their assorted wares on the street.

"They are funny, these police – always harassing us when they are on duty, only to come and buy from us when they are off duty," she complained scornfully.

While **X**'s mother fought her own fights, **X** was locked in his own struggle to free himself from his parents' past. On the morning on which he finally succeeded in breaking free from this stranglehold, **X** stood at the broken window of his bedroom, looking out over the troubled neighbourhood. The whiff of tear gas was unmistakable. In the distance, a pall of smoke rose in the direction of the Zimbabwe Grounds, where a protest rally was taking place. He contemplated it with an uneasy curiosity.

It had scarcely occurred to him that such strife could visit his own backyard of Fio, and, while he had always been certain about how he would react, now he realised that he was actually apprehensive. It was one thing to proselytise about a struggle in need of some fire in the safety of The Café, but quite another to be confronted by a struggle that not only spilled into his backyard but also threatened to invite itself into the room where he now stood transfixed. Soon the acrid sting of tear gas would penetrate the whole house, so he readied himself to go and meet it instead. With a towel still wet from the bath he had just taken, he made for the door. A poem – freshly composed and the paper neatly folded and tucked into the back pocket of his trousers – compelled him to go out there and perform. His name was not on the rally's programme, but he would surely find a way to be heard.

The house was in semi-darkness. His mother had locked the doors, closed all the windows and drawn the curtains, to give the impression that there was no one at home. As he passed her, she stopped him with a look.

"Where do you think you are going? Can't you see what is happening outside? Why don't you wait until we see the back of this thing?" His mother's questions always came in a salvo, that's how she came to be known as the PP – Public Prosecutor. "That wet towel of yours is not a magic charm. It will only protect your eyes against the tear gas but there are guns out there – *real* guns," she admonished him.

"Mama, the guns will never be fired because this is not a war zone. I have to go now because today is the anniversary of the Poetry Slam. You know I have to be there." He was not telling the truth, but his mother had no way of knowing this. She would never have let him go out of the house if she had known his real intentions. She knew how passionate her only son was about poetry, which she sometimes heard him reciting in his bedroom or in their tiny backyard, sometimes at odd hours in the dead of night. Aware that she could not win this time, she handed him the key, accompanied by a warning that was an instruction at the same time: "Be careful and be home early."

The stench that greeted him as he left the gate of their house made him nauseous. He jumped gingerly across the street to avoid landing in the puddles of raw sewage that flooded the plentiful potholes in the tarmac. Rivers of sewage flowed freely, manoeuvring their way past mountains of uncollected garbage. When the water supply was restored after one of the many outages, frequently sewage had accumulated and dried up in the crumbling sewer system. Unable to chart its usual course, the water, together with the offending waste, would find its way to freedom through overwhelmed manholes into the narrow streets, vegetable gardens and homes. The residents, now steeled into an unwilling self-sufficiency by many years of neglect, knew exactly how to deal with this menace. They dug trenches to redirect the offending waste away from their homes, only to see the obnoxious rivulets passed back to them like some kind of a fluid ball by their equally self-sufficient neighbours.

As he made his way towards the Zimbabwe Grounds, **X** thought about how only recently life had seemed a difficult but otherwise endurable daily grind. Now things were different. If a month ago you had to go looking for trouble, today trouble was all around – looking for you. It hung palpably in the air, and he was afraid.

The foreboding about the day's unfolding events was overpowering and yet enticing at the same time. Strains of U2's *Sunday Bloody Sunday* echoed in his head as he drew closer to the grounds. The throbbing, military beat was like guns popping in his head, persistent and lethal but appealing to his sense of adventure. To calm his frayed nerves, he hummed the little he remembered of the song, its chorus playing out like a horror movie in his head:

> 'Cause tonight we can be as one….
> Bodies strewn across the dead end street
> Sunday Bloody Sunday
> And the battle's just begun

There's many lost but tell me who has won?

The poignancy of the lyrics was at that point entirely lost on him; instead he was entertaining the possibility that maybe one day he might use the song as background music to the performance of a poem that was beginning to take shape in his head.

While wrapped up in this fantasy, **X** turned a street corner and stumbled into a squad of policemen in worn out blue jumpsuits, some armed with truncheons and others with automatic rifles, tear gas canisters menacingly strapped to their hips. His initial reaction was to walk right past them – eyes downcast – as if headed anywhere other than his intended destination. One of the policemen – he didn't look up to see which one – barked an instruction from behind the visor of his helmet: "Hey boy, go back home. It's cancelled."

X knew what the policeman meant, and he knew better than to argue with the tone of finality lacing the lawman's voice. After all, when a policeman said move, you moved. So he immediately turned, and retraced his steps, half running and not daring to looking back. When he was a safe distance away, he gathered the courage to steal a glance out of the corner of his eye and saw that the policemen already seemed oblivious of him, laughing heartily at something that appeared to be totally unrelated to the current circumstances. He could tell that they were not spoiling for a fight and were there only because they were required to be. He turned into a side road that would enable him to evade them and proceed to the grounds by another route.

He brushed aside this minor setback and hurried towards the grounds, listening intently for any sounds that might give away what was happening there. The sound of a whistle was unmistakable, commanding him to hurry up and be part of history. By now his brisk walk had broken into a jog, the sound of wailing sirens heightened his uneasy expectancy, and he sweated profusely from both the sweltering mid-morning heat and the anxiety.

The chanting was powerful and compelling even though **X** could barely make out the words. Suddenly the chanting crowd crashed into sight like a gigantic wave. It was clear that the crowd was not running towards something but away from something. For a moment he stood transfixed, awed by the sheer mass of people singing at the top of their voices. He could feel their energy lifting him, just like the audience at a poetry slam. As if on cue, he turned and started *toyi-toying* with them. He was now at the front of the crowd that marched resolutely in the direction of the policemen from his earlier encounter. To his surprise, the crowd burst into applause behind him, impressed by his enthusiasm and the image of Malcolm X emblazoned on the back of his T-shirt.

Fio, living up to its image as the cradle of militant resistance, was by now engulfed in a miasma of tear gas and smoke from burning debris. The suburb had degenerated into a war zone as angry youths blockaded the streets with anything they could find – evoking the grainy images of strife-torn places from the television news. Grey crowd control vehicles lumbered along the narrow streets, spraying jets of pressurised water into fleeing crowds, immobilising some while others simply ducked behind walls. Tear gas canisters whizzed through the air, menacingly pursuing protesters who responded with a hail of missiles – stones, sticks, bricks, garbage bins, broken bottles – anything that could be thrown. The canisters were quickly smothered with wet clothing and hurled back at the advancing policemen.

X was now in a frenzy as he threw stones, chanted slogans and sang songs he had neither heard nor sung before. The fear that had possessed him only a short while before vanished, leaving in its place a heady cocktail of courage and anger. The moment he had long awaited had arrived. He did not need to perform his poem – he was the poem.

The squad of policemen stood in a straight line across the street, their shields a wall meant to block the seemingly inexorable march of the crowd, but the prospect of being overpowered sent a wave of panic through their ranks. One of the policemen fired his gun into the air and ordered the crowd to disperse, but, sensing victory, the crowd pressed on. The gunman seemed unsure what to do next, unsettled by the glare of hundreds of eyes.

X threw his fist into the air to hurl his anger at the policemen but found only the stone in his hand. Then the policeman fired his gun. The sound of the gunshot and the searing pain in his chest hit X at the same time. He slumped to the ground and a pool of blood began to flow from his limp body. In the ensuing pandemonium, people trampled upon him as they fled in all directions. Their bloodied footprints were clear on the tarmac.

Later, someone covered X's face with his jacket and rummaged through his pockets to identify him. The only document he found was the neatly folded piece of paper in the back pocket, now stained with blood. The man started reading it; slowly enough to convey the gravity of the occasion but loudly enough for those who had gathered around the body to hear. His hands trembled with emotion as tears fell from his eyes onto the paper:

There is a scar on my soul
Etched by hit men in unmarked cars
Who arrive unceremoniously to disturb pre-dawn peace
To abduct my weary dreams
Ruthlessly shaking them wide-awake
In the dead of the night

There is a scar on my soul
Inflicted by black-suited, bloodshot-eyed terror,
That force-marches thoughts of freedom into grass-
                                    thatched hearts,
And burns them alive

There is a scar on my soul
Where free speech digs its own shallow grave,
And lies in it to await a silent death.
And freedom lies face down
And submits to sjamboks and iron bars

Repeatedly thrashed under the feet
This vision is all bloodied and walks with a heavy limp,
It is slowly going nowhere in particular
And its footsteps are scars on my soul

     At the bottom, **X** had written the date and put a large **X** underneath it.

Perhaps as an act of penance for letting **X** die, perhaps as a desperate bid to inherit the fiery creativity that **X** drew from this place, Nhamo himself started frequenting The Café. He swore that sometimes he couldn't tell the difference between his own life and the one he created for **X**, so one day he showed up to perform at the Poetry Slam, convinced that he was **X**. The audience did not boo him off the stage, but he could tell from the bored looks on their faces that they did not understand what he was trying to do, so he has recoiled to his dull life, doomed to play second fiddle to a figment of his own imagination.

Alone

Fungai Rufaro Machirori

I am looking at the milky zit on his upper lip and panicking about what to do if he lunges forward to kiss me.

He's saying a lot of things – how business is slowing and how he's looking at expanding into Kenya or Nigeria or somewhere else up north to keep up his profits.

I'm half listening; minimally sympathetic to his concerns, but even more worried about that pregnant pimple – the size of a large pinhead – that would surely pop and erupt if disturbed by a brush of my lips. What if it bursts and squirts its contents into my mouth? What if it bleeds and I am forced to taste his blood?

The thoughts are racing through my mind like the pistons of a well-oiled machine; perhaps too well greased.

Mildred would laugh if I told her about this, being the person who'd nicknamed me 'OCD Olivia', in honour of what she perceives to be the obsessive traits of my character.

My dear Obsessive Compulsive Disordered Olivia,
Here's hoping that the coming years aren't as crazy as the last few!!!

She'd written that into my 27th birthday card, with carefree loops punctuated generously by exclamation marks featuring cheeky smiley faces instead of full stops.

And the name had stuck.

In fact it's been years since that birthday card and Mildred maintains that it's the 'OCD' in me that explains why I am childless, unmarried and therefore somewhat unfulfilled – because when I pack cans of cola into the fridge, their labels have to face forwards at a slightly acute angle to the railing of the fridge door – an angle I've calculated to about 45 degrees; because I dutifully alternate the side of the bed I sleep on every second night for no other reason that I can explain but habit; because I live on the philosophy of women's liberation and never let a man settle the whole bill for anything; because I am picky about men to a point where I can do without them completely; and of course, because tonight Philemon's lonely pimple is pricking at my thoughts so intensely.

The truth be told, I don't think I am obsessive, compulsive or disorderly at all – I just like to be in control of things.

I am a 35-year old career woman and I've bought everything I own. I have surely earned the right to do things the way I like them done, regardless of what anyone else thinks or says.

Still, I can't deny that Mildred's words sometimes stick to my mind as though they have been glued there, or held down with office pins – with screaming pinheads of red and yellow; pinheads not quite the creamy colour sprouting out of Philemon's lip, distracting me once again.

He keeps talking as though he doesn't realise it even exists, as though he shaved and got dressed for our dinner date and never noticed the ghastly thing gawking back at him in the mirror.

But surely, he too has seen it and noted how disgusting it looks – a clot of yellowing milk festering in a capsule above his thick brown lips. It must be throbbing some sort of reminder to him of its existence, of its exponential expansion, as it gestates and breeds with more pus.

I decide that he must be ignoring it in the hope that I take no heed of its presence too.

"So anyway, yeah, that's what I'm thinking about doing in the near future. Watch this space!" Philemon lets out a throaty laugh that sounds like an awkward cough, then looks ahead out of the windscreen, into the endless expanse of blackness, interrupted by the blinks of a few semi-blind street lights. A choir of cicadas chirps and adds a chorus to the silence.

I am not amused and decide it's time to end this uncomfortable situation. But as I reach downwards to unclasp my seat belt, Philemon turns a quick right angle to face me. I immediately sense that he is expecting it – a warm moist good night kiss that would surely entail my sucking on that unpalatable zit that I have had to endure for the last two hours.

In anticipation, he reaches down to place a hand over mine. It is a big hand, the size of a goalkeeper's mitt, and the texture of the manila paper I've been making cue cards from for a work assignment. Out of the corner of my eye I perceive him slowly looking up hoping to meet my eyes ascending with his.

But they do not. Instead, I continue to look downwards at the clasp re-reading the word 'Press' on the red part of it. I want to press it and eject from my seat through the roof of the car like a pilot abandoning a plane that's about to combust into a fireball.

Philemon tries to move across, towards my down-turned face, ignoring the cringe that's quickly walking a path across my eyes and cheeks.

Suddenly, I press the bright red pause button in my mind.

"Stop!"

He is startled by the unexpected word and jerks away.

"I don't er... I don't get intimate on a first date. Sorry if I scared you."

My voice has become glassy.

"Oh. OK." The trio of whispered syllables emit from his mouth, releasing a warm gush of menthol I hadn't previously noticed on his breath.

Earlier in the night I'd noted similar dismay in his tone at my insistence on splitting the dinner bill right down the middle as though I was a skilled surgeon trained for such occasions. It was one of the few times throughout the meal that I had actually made eye contact with him, fearing the eruption of nausea at the sight of his pimple. How rude of him to make me endure such torture! He really should have rescheduled. And how much ruder of him to think that I would want to kiss him in such a state. My cold glassiness thaws and erupts into offended rage.

Still perplexed, Philemon replaces his hands on to the spongy steering wheel. If his gravelly face wasn't laced with such intricate ravines of sweat, I might have slapped him. But I don't want to part company taking *any* of his bodily fluids along with me.

"Good night," I say, facing the door on my side and pulling at its latch. "And next time you notice such a zit on your face, I recommend you rub some fresh garlic over it for a while. And if it doesn't disappear, just reschedule your date! It has really been off-putting!"

I close the car door with a swift shove and stomp off.

He'd have to be a glutton for humiliation to ever get back in touch with me.

My breasts are soft.

Not in that poetic way that romantics describe the touch and feel of their lover's chest; not in that youthful supple manner that you could write sonnets about.

My breasts are soft like a mushy loaf of freshly baked bread; like *sadza* that's been cooked so thin you can't actually pinch it into balls as you try to soak it with the soup of an accompanying relish. *Mbodza.*

In fact, my breasts aren't soft. They sag. When I lift my nipples upwards, a mess of fine wrinkles ripples across my skin like I'm pulling up a crumpled curtain.

My belly is becoming saggy too; runny jelly wobbling between my chest and thighs.

The mirror doesn't lie. Sadly, it can't be bribed to be deceptive. And just like me, it can be cold calculating glass that reflects back at you unfazed by the despondence it causes with its painful truths.

My nude form forces me to try to recall the last time anyone had seen me this way. I can count more months than my fingers yield – a full year and three months.

With no one to compare notes, I cannot even begin to trace the beginnings of these changes to my body. And therefore I must trust that the mirror is no liar, and that I am aging, secretly, beneath my clothes.

I start to think about Simba.

He knew this body when my breasts peaked like chocolate meringues that would melt so easily within his kisses; when the cellulite intrusion had not yet colonised all parts of me, before the 'OCD' tag set in thick and I was that supple feisty-yet-yielding young woman.

What would he think if he saw me today, now – so distinctly jaded by time? Was he not the cause of the loss of that girl anyway?

Time.

"How much longer do you want to be alone?" My mother's words bolt from the creases of my thoughts, momentarily taking me hostage.

"I am not alone. I travel to fascinating places, have cosmopolitan friends and read enlightening books. I do work that is essential, analysing and formulating development policies and I get invited to speak at international conferences and workshops. I own my own house, as well as the black Mercedes Benz parked in the garage *and* I will have my PhD soon." I recite the sales pitch that my mother so richly despises.

Ironically, I *am* alone in my bedroom as I shout those emphatic words, vanquishing thoughts of her many questions. And so no one else hears the words ricochet off the mirror and fall back onto my face like the good hard slap I had wanted to give Philemon.

I feel the sting.

Since Simba, my mother has been hassling me to get married and finally give her some grandchildren: she says it's getting embarrassing for her to explain to relatives why I am so 'old' and yet still unmarried and childless.

I remind her there are other things to life than marriage and children, hence the elaborate sales pitch. Whenever I say it out, my mother sighs through her withered cheeks, clutching at her heart as though fearful it will explode.

Sometimes I feel just as weary as she does.

Travelling is amazing, but not always on a round trip booked for one. What I wouldn't give to have been able to ride up to the peak of the Eiffel Tower with someone more special than the hosting French delegation for our conference that lovely summer when the Parisian fantasy finally came true. What I wouldn't do to be guaranteed a bunch of roses and a box of chocolates each Valentine's Day, an unexpected call on a late night in the office.

And yes, my body is giving way to gravity and time as it should – but long before I have had the chance to dance it through the different phases of womanhood, and not just a single era stalled because of one man's memory.

My duvet cover is peeled half-open and my pillow is dented by the tome on gender and economic development that I am reading to prepare a bibliography for an academic article.

Tonight, I'll be reading and then sleeping on the left side of the bed, allowing my mind to wander every now and then to thoughts of finding someone who could understand this crazy thing I do with swapping sides of the bed every second night.

"So how did it go?"

Mildred makes a point of coming in after lunchtime the following day as she thinks Philemon might have stayed over the previous night.

I am tackling a crusty stain on the stove that has been irritating me for the last two days and trying to distract myself from her prying. A heavy smell of sourness fills the kitchen from the pot of rice that's grown mouldy overnight and now nestles in a disposable bag in the bin.

"You know, this dating agency thing doesn't seem to be my cup of tea. We just didn't gel."

It'd been Mildred's idea to give Heart2Heart, the dating agency that was advertising fervently in the local press, a shot. After all, they promised 'a match made in heaven for even the loneliest'.

Mildred had been more excited than I ever was, setting up the appointment with the agency, paying for the service fees and even filling out the forms on my behalf.

Olivia Gavi. 35 years old. 1.73m. Dark brown complexion. Professional woman. Never married. No children. Seeking man 35-45 years old who must be a professional, as well as single (divorcés and men with children are welcome).

This wasn't what I really wanted – to be parading my life around a matchmaking agency – but Mildred was certain that this was what I needed.

I always finish work late, even carrying some of it home. Therefore, I barely ever find time for a night out or for socialising, favouring instead the quiet familiarity of the walls of my office.

"You'll thank me when you meet and marry Mr Right," Mildred beamed as she heartily wrote out the prerequisites of a possible suitor.

Finding Mr Right through a dating agency? I wished Mildred could understand the absurdity of the suggestion. And finally, through Philemon, I had a clear example why.

"So you ditched the man over a pimple, which, mind you, is something that he has no control over!"

"Mildred, it was revolting! And for him to even think that I would kiss him was just disrespectful!"

She lets out a sigh as she shakes her heard bemusedly. She will never say it but I know what she is thinking, beyond even the 'OCD' theories. My best friend is worried that, like the pot of rice that's quietly rotting away in my kitchen bin, I too will soon grow an offensive mould that will drive everyone away from me.

My cell phone vibrates in its silent setting during a management meeting on Monday morning. The digits are unfamiliar to me and, after the drawn meeting, I return a call to the number.

"Heart2Heart Matchmaking Consultants. Irene speaking, can I help you?"

I wince as I recall the story behind the missed call. Irene asks for my name, which I surrender hesitantly.

"Miss Gavi, yes we did try to call you to inform you of a match between your details and those of two of our clients. The information has already been sent to the email address that we used previously."

I am not sure whether to thank her or to feel intruded upon.

With Philemon having been such a disaster, I had been half-expecting him to report me to the agency and have me banned for inflicting untold humiliation on him.

But perhaps he took my advice to heart and realised that small omissions, such as lack of attention to one's physical appearance, might be the reason why he's 43 and still single.

Talk about the kettle calling the pot black. I know. I know.

But I am somehow curious to log on to my email account and read a bit more about the matches – two whole men whose spheres of interest coincide with my own.

I manage to say a soft thank you to the bubbly young woman before hanging up and logging on. And sure enough there is an email from the agency signed off in red by the company's executive director, Bertha-Lee Hove, who states, "Love will find you in your darkest hour. Shine a light towards it."

Am I, I wonder, in my darkest hour? I surely must be if I can use office time to check out possible suitors on my laptop. What would Tari, my personal assistant, say or think if she caught me in the act? Strangely, I feel as though I am watching soft porn on office time.

The attachment to the email downloads and my screen lights up with the photographs of two very different looking men. The first is called Shadreck. His bio states that he is 44 years old, divorced, a father of two, and a senior advisor for a law firm who's looking to settle down again. His accompanying photograph shows a light skinned man with a shaggy mottled beard and balding head.

Quickly, I glance to my right at the closed door and look down at the slit it leaves before the floor to check if there are any approaching feet. I only see vacant light and take this as my cue to continue on to the next candidate – Melvin.

He is 38 years old, never married, childless and a self-employed businessman looking for the same things as Shadreck. He is smiling in his photograph, which immediately startles me. His complexion is much darker than Shadreck's and his lips are thick and wide. And his eyes are… his eyes are… Simba's own wide washed-out brown colour. The dimples that his smile dots into his cheeks are also so much like Simba's that it sends a shiver down my spine instantly.

But how? Could it be...

Before I can contemplate any further, a loud shriek suddenly interrupts my thoughts.

It is the telephone blaring loudly like an attention-seeking child. The sound instantly spreads a surge of panic throughout me and I quickly close the lid of my laptop.

"Your 11 o'clock meeting is just about to begin," says Tari on the other end of the line once I pick up.

"Thanks Tari," I reply abstractedly, still disturbed by what I think I have just seen.

In the end, it was Mildred – and more embarrassingly, her husband, Tatenda – who'd persuaded me to go for a second date. Usually, Tatenda stayed out of women's business so I was certain that it was Mildred who'd coerced him to say something.

"Men mellow with time so you've got nothing to worry about. The older we become, the wiser we get," he said, visibly self-conscious of his presence in such a discussion.

I wanted to raise the example of Philemon whom I still deemed to be puerile beyond words. But I realised I would be giving Mildred more fuel for her 'OCD' fire and therefore kept silent.

It wasn't that I completely disagreed with Tatenda anyway. It was just the manner in which the process was being facilitated that made me uneasy. Was I really this desperate – desperate enough to pick and choose a man from a catalogue? A man I couldn't even be certain was being honest about himself?

"Guys, my life is fulfilled. Don't worry about me so much. Everything in its own time."

Mildred rolled her eyes and noticed my clasping and unclasping of my wristwatch. She'd labelled it one of the 'compulsions' she said I suffered when I felt mildly irritated.

"Don't be such a ninny. You aren't getting any younger and if you keep working as hard as you do, all your eggs will shrivel up prematurely!"

I wasn't sure I even wanted children, but everyone prescribed them as the elixir to all of life's problems. Tari, herself also a mother, always teased that I wouldn't take my work so seriously if I just settled down and had kids. The intensity that coloured my working hours would be saved for something more meaningful instead, she said.

I wondered if this meant that she wasn't putting her all into her work and wondered even more when I caught her navigating her Facebook page at her desk on innumerable occasions. Didn't she understand how important advocating for reform to gender-insensitive policy and legislation was? Didn't she realise that some people had to immerse themselves so completely in the cause if any gains were to be had?

I knew that most of my workmates thought of me as a paradox. How could I fight for women's rights to community of property in marriage, to maternal wellbeing during childbirth, to avert patriarchal practices such as domestic violence and *kugara nhaka;* how could I fight on their behalf when I didn't know what it felt like to be in their shoes? I knew they thought of me as a detached half-woman who spoke from theory and not everyday lived experiences.

My mother would have been pleased if I had told her I worked amid such acerbic forces. More fuel for yet another fire raging against me.

And yet somehow, I understood it; their desire to contort my life into the prescribed mould that every woman was supposed to fill out perfectly. That was culture wasn't it? That system that places marriage and motherhood on the priority lists of every woman, regardless of whether or not they desire them. And ironically, it was those very systems of thought that we arrived at work each weekday to fight.

I sometimes wondered too if Mildred understood me as well as I thought she did.

She and Tatenda had been married since we'd graduated from university and, ever since then, she'd extolled the virtues of marriage no end, even though it was plain to see what a great sacrifice she'd made for this union.

Mothering four children almost consecutively had cost her opportunities for career growth – opportunities that I had been able to take with unbridled conviction. At 35, I owned property and a wealth of knowledge and experiences. Mildred, on the other hand, was still in a junior staff position in the organisation that she'd been working for for almost 10 years – no one sees a woman in her baby-making prime as a valuable office asset.

I didn't want to be like that. And I was grateful that I never would be.

I still sometimes wondered how differently life might have turned out if Simba had stayed with me. Could love have softened me to the point where all I wanted was to knit booties and brood over babies? Could I, like Mildred, have tucked my life's dreams to sleep for the sake of a family?

But there was no use in thinking about what could never be, especially now with Tatenda and Mildred staring at me expectantly, waiting for a response.

"OK, for the conservation of my endangered eggs, I will humour you two and go on another date."

And right then I decided that if for nothing else but natural curiosity and a chance to transpose the dead onto the living, I would choose Melvin as my second try.

"I love it when you wear those jeans."

"Stop it Simba!"

It's the last warning I will give him because I am really trying to concentrate on the movie we are watching.

Neria is the story of a woman whose husband dies leaving her with a myriad traditional customs to deal with – from inheritance of property to being inherited as a second wife by his brother.

We are only 19 years old but Neria's story stabs at my conscience so deeply that I decide to devote myself to working in gender and development that very moment.

Simba continues to chomp away loudly at his popcorn, sensing that I don't want to make out in the cinema house this time.

"What would you do if we got married and-"

"Married?" I stop Simba before he can continue with his train of thought. The taxi driver who he's hired to drive us back to campus lets out a shortened chuckle that sounds like a hiccup.

"Hey! Let me finish. What would you do if we got married and I died like that woman's husband? Would you let my brother take you over?"

"Firstly, there is no guarantee that we will ever get married. Secondly I don't know that if we did get married I wouldn't be driven to death first – through suicide. And lastly, I would never allow myself to be used as a pawn to appease your relatives. So no, I wouldn't let your brother take me over like a car."

"That's a feisty one you have there!" The taxi driver can't help but add his two cents to the conversation, watching us go on through his rear view mirror.

"I know that, *mudhara.* Dynamite! But one day she's going to be my wife."

A flutter goes through my stomach. Simba seems so certain and determined to make us last forever, to ensure that I am always his.

"Time will tell," I say, cautioning my thoughts against something that is still so far away in my mind.

He smiles back at me, his eyes remaining sincere. "You know I'm right. You'll always be mine."

That memory hadn't risen to my consciousness in many months. But I am currently thinking about what I promised Simba that day all that time ago.

He and I would have beaten Mildred and Tatenda to the altar if he hadn't died so unexpectedly; a 24-year-old young man in perfect physical shape suffering a heart attack and dying in his sleep.

How could all our dreams for the future have gone to bed one night and not woken up the next morning?

It shattered me for many months, for many dark weeks when I considered taking my own life and reuniting with him. And as I slowly pieced together the fragments of my soul, I decided that love was far too painful to pursue ever again because it could leave you without even saying goodbye.

I therefore buried Simba and the dream, shovelling him away to the deepest place within myself, covering him up with a career I could now pursue without reservation. And while everyone else around me wed and gave life, I immersed myself deeper into the world of rights and freedoms, of activism on behalf of the voiceless women whose pain I infused with my own. Pain did not know circumstances or causes. It was all the same.

My mother, Mildred, Tatenda – they all did not understand what Simba's pain meant to me. Did they really think that life gave us all a spare soul mate, like the spare button stitched into the hem of a new coat in case the original fell out?

"I am not alone. I travel to fascinating places, have cosmopolitan friends and read enlightening books."

Over time the pitch had grown until it became the plug that stopped everyone seeing the hole in my heart.

"This next guy will be better. I can feel it."

Mildred's words echo within my head. She means well – I know that.

But I want to tell her something she will find bizarre. Perhaps I should just show her the picture of Melvin and ask her if I'm being crazy for thinking he looks so strikingly, so poignantly like Simba.

And then I can tell her about the promise that I made to him over 15 years ago; that I wouldn't ever marry his brother like they tried to force Neria to.

Yes I know Melvin and Simba aren't brothers, I'll say. And yes, I need to move on with my life. But… but I still love Simba with all of my heart and everything else within me. And going out with anyone so similar to him – could I possibly handle it?

And then I know Mildred will talk about 'OCD' and maybe even say that I need grief counselling or something similar.

"It's not normal to still feel this way after so many years. Go on with your life because nothing can ever bring Simba back."

The voice is at first Mildred's and then morphs into my mother's.

"But I am not alone! I travel to fascinating places, have cosmopolitan…."

I can't remember how it all ends right now. I don't want to.

I don't need to because, in my heart, I know I will never be alone.

They are Coming

Christopher Mlalazi

Arms stretched over his head, and his mouth open in a half yawn, Lungisani stands at the gate, looking down Khumbulani Street. A thin stream of effluent snakes its way along the far edge of the street, almost as if on tiptoe.Although its stench pervades the morning air, Lungisani is now used to it as the waste has been flowing unchecked for over a month, and so he is not bothered.

Houses crowd the street from both sides, and women, bent over, sweep their yards, tidying them up for the new day. A radio blasts *mbaqanga* music somewhere and accompanying the music are the raised voices of children. By their shouts, Lungisani guesses they are playing 'hit me'.

His eyes blurred with tears brought about by yawning, the shirtless Lungisani can see that conversations are jumping across and along the street between the women as they sweep. He cannot catch what is being said, but can only see the accompanying gestures with the free hand, or the sweep, as dust clouds, like speech bubbles on the walls of his classroom at school, rise over each of these women.

One, two, three, four, five, as Lungisani counts the women with his eyes, the phrase 'five mothers are sweeping and gossiping' jumps into his mind. One fat mother and four very thin mothers are sweeping the five yards of their five houses in autumn. Suddenly, one of the women stops sweeping. The fat one. Still bent over, she looks in his direction and then her body jerks upright.

Even at this distance, Lungisani can see that her mouth is wide open, as if in shock, or something close to that. Then her face snaps to her thin neighbour, who also jerks upright, and both women look in his direction. One by one, from both sides of the street, the women straighten up, and they all look towards Lungisani.

Lungisani's eyes remain fixed on the women. With mouths open wide, it is as if the women are singing a song, the kind sung by *izinyanga* and their mediums. It looks as if they will leap into a furious dance, their grass sweeps flailing in his direction in superstitious denial.

There is nothing wrong with our family, he wants to shout at them. Please don't look at me like that.

"They are coming!" A hoarse cry erupts from behind him, startling him from his thoughts.

Lungisani whirls around. A man is running hard towards him from up the street. Lungisani gapes as he realises that the women had not in fact been staring at him, but past him at this man. The man's white shirt is in tatters that flap in the wind, just like that of the scarecrow that his mother has erected in the family maize field in the bush behind the township. Lungisani instantly recognises him. It is Mr Nkani, the Grade 7A teacher at his school. The one who gave his brother Persuade a thorough beating when he found him with a pack of cigarettes in his school bag last year. Lungisani has seen little of his brother since Persuade left school, and home, a few months ago. Mr Nkani's face is plastered on posters all around the township, posters that are tied to trees, to electricity and telephone poles, and stuck on walls at the shopping centre where his father works. People say he belongs to the opposition, and that they will vote for him in the elections next week.

"Hide!" Mr Nkani shouts as he races past. "They are coming." Blood flows down the side of Mr Nkani's face, and the tatters of his shirt are also streaked with blood.

"Lungisani," screams his mother through the open window of the kitchen. "*Wena*! Come in at once."

Tatenda's chubby face peeps from beside that of his mother, his eyes open as wide as the centres of two ring doughnuts.

The street is now empty. The sweeping women and the fleeing Mr Nkani have all disappeared but, in the distance, the *mbaqanga* music still blares and the voices of the children still call out.

"It's hot inside," Lungisani replies in a sulky voice, as he pulls up his saggy shorts.

"Lungisani," MaNdlovu shouts again. "This child!" she continues to no-one and her face disappears from the window.

Suddenly Lungisani sees them boil from around the corner from which Mr Nkani had appeared. They are running hard, harder than Mr Nkani had been, a group of youths wielding stones and sticks, yelling and whistling.

Just then, MaNdlovu appears behind Lungisani. With both hands she snatches him up and carries him into the house, as if he does not weigh anything at all.

They stand at the closed window of the kitchen, peeping towards the gate, their faces a medley of expressions – fear on that of Lungisani's mother, who knows fully what the Green Bombers represent, anger on that of Lungisani, who still wants to be outside, and wide eyed excitement on that of Tatenda, who is happy to watch the action from the safety of the window. Lungisani's friend Tatenda, who lives next door, is seven, three years younger than Lungisani.

As the Green Bombers flash past the gate. Lungisani knows that they never run like that without wanting to catch somebody. Last week, he and Tatenda had seen the Green Bombers chasing a man and a woman who wore opposition party T-shirts. They had caught the man and the woman in front of them and beaten them until they were covered in blood and lay on the ground, just like dead people.

A moment later, Lungisani has escaped from the house and is crouching at the gate. The Green Bombers have disappeared just as Mr Nkani had done, and all he can see is a cloud of dust that floats in the air. He straightens as, one by one, people start coming out of their gates and stare in the direction of the chase. No one speaks. The *mbaqanga* music has stopped, as have the voices of the playing children, as if the chase in the street has gobbled them all up.

Then, unexpectedly, there are screams from along the street. The people at the far end dash back inside their homes, and doors bang closed like gunshots.

The Green Bombers appear from around the corner, running hard back towards Lungisani. This time the Green Bombers are not chasing, but are fleeing for dear life. Once again Lungisani finds himself unceremoniously carried aloft in his mother's arms, and deposited back into the kitchen.

"Stubborn!" MaNdlovu shouts at him. She slaps him as if to emphasize her point and slams the door closed, quickly locking it. She rushes to the window to look out, Lungisani and Tatenda beside her. The Green Bombers zip past the window, headed back the way they had come. There is a lull, and then another mob rushes past, hard on the heels of the Green Bombers.

This new group chasing the Green Bombers is yelling and whistling and throwing stones just as the Green Bombers had been doing when they were chasing Mr Nkani. The group is comprised of a mixture of men, women and children, and, tagging behind, is the township stray, Ginger, normally a timid dog, but now barking and chasing with the others.

Mr Nkani, still in his torn and blood-stained shirt, leads this group, snatching up stones from the ground and throwing them in the direction of the Green Bombers, as if he is lobbing grenades.

Without a thought, Lungisani swiftly unlocks and opens the door and runs to the gate. More people run past, chasing the Green Bombers; so many people, as if the whole township has rallied. Lungisani joins the chase. Even though he is small, he overtakes some of the crowd. Without warning, the chasing crowd shudders to a halt. Some scream in fear, turn around and start running back the way they have come. Lungisani finds himself standing in the front line, facing the Green Bombers, who have turned back.

The two groups confront each other across a small stream of effluent that cuts across the street. An uneasy quiet descends.

Lungisani stares at one of the Green Bombers. This youth, slim bodied, is in the same green T-shirt as the rest of the Green Bombers, and wears a green floppy hat. The brim of the hat falls over his face, concealing much of it from view. In his hand is the national flag on a short staff. The youth stares intently back at Lungisani, his head tilted for a clearer view from under the brim of the hat.

A half brick is held in Lungisani's hand.

"Lungisani!" His mother's cry comes from behind him.

The spell is broken.

Yells erupt from the Green Bombers, and stones start to fly. One just misses Lungisani's head. He raises his arm to throw the half brick, but his mother rushes towards him to snatch his hand and shake the missile to the ground. Her furious face hovers over him like a dark cloud. She spanks him on his buttocks, and drags him back towards their home, with stones raining all around them.

As soon as they reach home, Lungisani rushes to the window and stares out at the street. The stone-throwing adversaries have all disappeared.

A bicycle skids into their yard and falls over in a cloud of dust. A man in dark overalls leaps up from the dust and, a moment later, Lungisani's father is standing beside them at the window. The sleeves of his overalls are rolled up, and he is inspecting his grazed elbows with glue-encrusted fingers.

"You are not hurt?" MaNdlovu asks him, concern on her brow.

"Not much," Ngwenya replies in a gruff voice. "Just grazed elbows from the bicycle fall."

"I feared for you," MaNdlovu says. She is still out of breath, her chest heaving beneath the old purple nightdress she is wearing.

"What happened at the bottle store today can never be talked about," Ngwenya says in a disturbed manner as he beats dust from his overalls. He is a big-bodied man, whose sagging cheeks show the ravages of a hard life.

"*Shuwa shuwa*, what does this government want us to do?" MaNdlovu points a finger towards the street. "What is happening out there, please people tell me?"

"We have not seen anything yet, I tell you." An ominous tone hangs over Ngwenya's words, as if what he sees in the future is too dark to even think about.

MaNdlovu shakes her head. "What happened at the bottle store?"

"I had gone there to look for somebody who sells cheap heels after I failed to get them in the factories this morning," Ngwenya starts his story. Lungisani and Tatenda look at him attentively, just as MaNdlovu. "Then Mr Nkani appeared, with the Green Bombers sitting on his tail. His shirt was torn, and he had blood all over."

"We also saw him," MaNdlovu says. "They passed right in front of our gate."

"We have always told that man to leave what he is doing," Ngwenya continues. "Mark my words, it will bring trouble to our township, but he refuses to listen. And look at what is happening now."

MaNdlovu claps her hands softly in reply, but does not say anything.

"Mr Nkani fled inside the bottle store, and came out a moment later with his friends and they chased the Green Bombers away, now with many from the township people joining in."

"We saw them passing here," Tatenda exclaims. "Ginger was chasing too and barking whoowu whoowu behind them." Tatenda barks for effect, his body bent over and his hands balanced on his knees. "But he can't bite people, he is a coward."

"Then the Green Bombers turned back to confront the people," Ngwenya continues. He lays his hand on Tatenda's head, who stands beside him. None of them has yet sat down.

"They turned back almost in front of our yard," MaNdlovu puts in, a stricken look on her face. "Ngwenya, you must do something about your child Lungisani, he is so stubborn. He was standing outside the gate when stones were flying everywhere, he could have been hurt. I had to pull him back inside the house. He is disobedient, just look at him!" She glares at Lungisani.

"Lungisani," Tatenda says, putting his hand over his mouth to titter behind it.

"Lungisani, you must listen to your mother." Ngwenya clicks his tongue at Lungisani, and removes his hand from Tatenda's head. "Do you want to see how I am when I am angry?" His voice begins to rise in anger. "Don't you know that the militia is dangerous and you might get hurt?"

Lungisani's head is cast down, his eyes fixed on his toes.

Ngwenya turns to MaNdlovu, and with a lowered voice says, "But later the people turned back again and chased the Green Bombers away. They have fled back to their base."

"They did not pass this way a second time," MaNdlovu replies.

"They went in a different direction." Ngwenya points a finger towards the back door. "Two rows behind our line of houses."

"They were defeated then. Good." There is exultation in MaNdlovu's voice.

"But only temporarily, you don't know them, Lungisani's mother. Those boys are very cheeky, as if they are fed on black termites."

"*Mayi-we*! They will come back tonight. These elections. I hate them. It wasn't like this at Independence."

"Because then we had a common enemy, the white regime. Now it is our government versus the people, the war has changed complexion."

"What about our children?"

"You can ask the President that. Has there been any sign of Persuade?"

"Nothing."

"I saw him," Lungisani says, looking up at his father.

"When – where?" Ngwenya almost stammers. Both parents look expectantly at Lungisani.

"Today."

"Where – answer my question, *mani*!" Ngwenya almost shouts.

"Please don't shout at the child," MaNdlovu says in a low voice. She looks at Lungisani. "Where did you see your brother, Lungisani?"

"Persuade was with the Green Bombers," Lungisani speaks reluctantly. "He was wearing a hat and carried a flag."

There is silence in the room.

"He wasn't with them, Lungisani," MaNdlovu finally says in a soft voice. "I saw the Green Bombers. You are mistaken, you saw somebody else who looks like your brother."

"I saw him." There is a stubborn note in Lungisani's voice.

"Don't speak back to your mother!" Ngwenya shouts at Lungisani. "I will hit you if you tell lies."

"Please no." MaNdlovu looks at her husband, concern on her face.

Lungisani darts to the door, quickly opens it and dashes out. The door bangs closed behind him.

Mr Pothole

Diana Charsley

"So there goes our Minister of Roads," announced Mrs Moyo. I glanced sideways at her, smiling politely but saying nothing, as I tossed a clod of clay into the grave. It glanced off the walls of the hole and shattered as it hit the coffin. She snorted in response to my lack of reply and joined her noisy friends while I stepped back and watched the gloss of the coffin dust over with gritty tokens from the procession of mourners. They drifted away and the cemetery grew quiet as the buses followed each other like flying ants to the main road. Funny, I thought, as I watched the remaining men filling the grave, this is so much like the work to which Jeremiah had given his recent life. Jeremiah Sithole: compelled prophet driven to put things right; ineffectual; the butt of beerhall jokes; my friend, neighbour and confidante.

I did not want to go to the wake, to hear the pop-psychology of loose-lipped drinkers theorizing about his behaviour. Neither did I want to go back to the house, and the road nearby – especially the road. I shambled towards my scruffy car and struggled to unlock it. Getting in I shut the door and sat motionless until the sticky heat forced me to unwind the window and get going. Driving slowly towards town I looked for something to dispel the heaviness I was feeling. Instead, standing on the side of the road, was the man who wandered up and down the roads in greasy rags and hessian mask. His chest was bare and a full-length coat flapped about him as he held up a smoking paint-pot, filled with smouldering grass and twigs, like some doomsday prophet. He stared at me, through me.

Driving past the sports club and its congested car park – the venue for the wake – I glanced towards it and chose to drive on until I noticed Caroline, Jeremiah's daughter, in the grip of the legendary Mrs Moyo. That bloody woman! I swung round and, after squeezing my car between two SUVs, hurried to rescue Caroline.

"Caroline, dear child, where is your brother? Let's go find him," I said, using the first words that came into my head that could draw her away. Mrs Moyo glowered at me.

"He's inside," she replied, quickly linking her arm through mine, enabling her release. We pushed our way towards the bar, through the crowd jostling for food. We parted thinning bamboo curtains to find Caroline's brother Themba alone in the gloom, drawing patterns on his glass of beer.

"Themba," I said as I waved to the barman for drinks.

"Hello neighbour," he murmured, not looking up. I had been their neighbour for twenty years, watching the two of them grow up.

"Not any more, I suppose," continued Themba, "now we are living in London, catching trains to work, work, work for money, money, money."

"So all the people here can enjoy our hospitality," added Caroline, looking through the spaces made by missing strands in the curtain at mourners fighting over the last chicken legs. "Well, better to have them busy over there than coming in here to console us. Outside the church was enough. All those people saying, 'How sad' and, 'Be strong', reminding us of how successful Baba once was. Most of them I'd never seen in my life before. Come for the freak-show I suppose."

"And the advice," said Themba. "Do you know that Mrs Moyo told me to go for regular check-ups. Does she think I will go the same way as Baba?"

"What does she know?" I replied. "Now that she's a nurse aide she thinks we should call her Doctor Moyo. But she wasn't there was she, Themba? She had to rely on gossip and assumptions. But we were there when it all started."

"When Jojo nearly got run over," whispered Caroline.

"Sitting in that pothole in the middle of the road," murmured Themba.

"The driver screamed at Baba, thinking he was the father," I added. Little Jojo had been about two then. He had found a way to open the gate. His mother worked for the family in exchange for accommodation in the staff quarters.

"I've had enough of this place," said Themba, standing up suddenly. He stared at the gritty, stained bar table, then scowled at the noisy crowd outside, "Take us home please, Uncle."

We slipped through the crowd unnoticed. A large car, for large people, had squeezed into a space on the driver's side of my car. I had to unlock the passenger door and slide across to the driver's seat, carefully negotiating the gear lever. The other two clambered in. I wanted to explain why a former managing director was driving such a heap, but the time did not seem right, so, crashing the gears, I reversed and headed towards their home. With the sun on the road, the afternoon traffic against us, and the potholes boiling clouds of dust I could barely see to drive.

"Watch out!" Caroline yelled. Simultaneously I saw an SUV bearing down on us as it overtook an oncoming *kombi*. I swung the car off the road barely avoiding a head-on collision. Then, through the dust in front of us, the same wild man I'd seen earlier loomed, his smoking pot held high as if he were about to smash the windscreen with it. I wrenched the wheel again, just missing him. Skidding to a stop I wiped the sweat off my face and looked back to check his condition. He hadn't moved. Together with the dust, the smoke from his pot caught the sun, forming an aura round his head. The drivers behind us hooted impatiently. "What is the matter with this place? Has everyone gone crazy?" choked Caroline. We continued the journey, unable to speak.

As we entered our street I clenched the steering wheel and felt my neck muscles tighten into a headache, I really hated this road. The two with me fidgeted uneasily. As I stopped at the gate, Themba got out and scraped it open. Parking the car outside the kitchen door I waited for him to catch up while Caroline went to the kitchen door and tugged it open. She filled the kettle for tea and turned it on while we sat down at the formica kitchen table. Themba rubbed his face with his hand then rattled his fingers on the table before folding his arms.

"The only good thing about being back here is that people can pronounce our surname 'Sithole' properly," he said. "Back in UK it's 'Sit-hole' or 'Sith-ough-l', they've never heard of an aspirated 'h' and they think every language has a silent 'e'." Caroline nodded, rolling her eyes. "London isn't much fun but at least we're anonymous there. Here we're the kids of the crazy man who heard voices that told him to fill in potholes. Mr Pothole, Minister of Roads they call him, though not to our faces. People smile when they see us coming and part like the Red Sea only to close into groups of gossip as we pass," Themba continued.

"I was fifteen when he started to talk to himself," said Caroline. "That was the end of inviting friends home from school. I hated him. I blamed him for ruining my life. One moment he was my hero, funny and clever, the father all my friends wished they had. The next he was this dirty, dishevelled person who didn't even recognise me. When I spoke to him he would look right through me and say something nonsensical. I told Mama she should divorce him."

"It was more like he was answering someone, someone inside his head," added Themba. "He seemed to be listening, then he would nod his head as if he had heard something important. Then he would go through the house and garden putting things in piles or in lines. Sometimes it seemed like he could not carry out the instructions he was getting, he would get agitated and start all over again, only making more of a mess and getting more upset. But after the Jojo incident it was potholes, day in and day out."

"Then mother left," added Caroline. "She said she was going to join her family down south and get a job to earn real money. Do you think it was my fault for telling her to get a divorce, Uncle?"

I shook my head gently, wishing I could ease her pain. "And then we left too. I know we were condemned for leaving him but we couldn't take it." Caroline stared out the window blinking rapidly. "Sorry, we left you to look after him, running away like rats from a burning field."

"It was easier for me," I said, "not being direct family and living next door. I had known your father all his life and it felt right that I should be the one to care for him, not that that was always possible. It was difficult to watch a fine man end up clothed in rags with nothing but a shovel for a friend. You know, in a way, maybe we are just as crazy as him."

"What do you mean?" said Themba, suddenly defensive.

"Well, let's look at it this way, when we have problems we try and find solutions, we take some form of action. Often what we do is not effective and even makes the problem worse. Take drinkers, for example, while they drink the problem goes away, but when they sober up the problem is still there, often exacerbated by their solution. As for us, we all run away in some way, trying to put some distance between ourselves and the problem. In a way your father tackled the problem head on. Maybe it helped him cope with his affliction. It was like he was on a mission. After he was blamed for Jojo being on the road – playing in a pothole so deep that a little boy sitting in it seemed more like a large bird than a child – it seemed that he was going to make it his business to prevent it happening to anyone else. He lived up to his title: Mr Pothole, Minister of Roads."

"Thanks for trying to make us feel better, but you make him sound as though he made a conscious decision to lead that lifestyle. Hey Caro, how goes the tea? Did you remember to turn that thing on?" Caroline gave her brother a rude sign as she got up.

"Oh great! No power. Again. At least that's one thing we don't have to put up with overseas," she said as she returned to the kitchen table. "I do see what Uncle is getting at though. Us two are living in a country with no family, covering distances from here to Gweru to get to work. In winter we get up in the dark and leave work in the dark, working at jobs where we know we'll never get promotion. And we're too scared to have kids. Is that crazy or what? I know Baba was driven by his voices but maybe he did save lives by what he did. I can't say that about the work I do."

"Maybe, but your work won't get you killed," said Themba. "What exactly happened, Uncle? We've never been told the full story." Themba searched my face. "You were first there, weren't you?"

I sighed heavily. "Yes, I usually came to check the house a couple of times a week. Jojo's mother still cleaned and cooked for him, but only while he was out. She had to make sure that she left everything exactly as it was, so as not to upset him. Well, I looked around and everything seemed fine so I went back over the fence to my house and headed off to work. Just round the corner a trench had been dug across half the road – another of those hazards we are used to. It seemed to have been half-filled with dark-brown soil. As I drove cautiously toward the trench I saw a shovel on the road. It was Jeremiah's. I would have recognised it anywhere: the handle wired together, the battered blade. I turned cold. Suddenly realising what the newly laid soil was, I put on my hazard lights and walked towards the trench. It was him. His body was face-down and filled the trench perfectly. Tyre tracks had dented his back. I couldn't figure how it happened that he should land just so. There were no brake-marks."

"The police just said it was a hit-and-run," said Themba. "How come you didn't tell us this before?"

"Tell you in front of the official mourners? So they could sneak off with a tasty morsel like mongrels snatching food from a child?"

"You're right, Uncle, we never had a moment's peace. Poor Baba," said Caroline blowing her nose, "I wonder if he even knew it was coming? A pothole for a grave."

Driving to the airport the next day we found ourselves with little to say and, once their luggage was cleared, Caroline and Themba chose to go through to the departure lounge. We hugged and I left. Driving slowly back to town through the ubiquitous roadblocks towards the city centre, I thought of my time with Jeremiah, wishing for our childhood when we proudly herded goats, and showed off our skills to anyone passing by. In the centre of town I had to slow down for pedestrians. It was Sunday and people were going to church. And there was Mrs Moyo, clearly visible, outside Faithful Followers Fellowship, sheathed in neon orange from turban to toe. As usual she was the centre of attention. She was trying to get the doomsday prophet to move along, without touching him, to move away from her church's entrance. Shaking my head I chuckled and gave him a thumbs-up as I drove past.

The Accidental Hero

Murenga Joseph Chikowero

I grinned. I could have thrown away the shameful crate of eggs, run off and caught the first *kombi* back to college. But I didn't. I stood there for a long minute like a naked giant. Following my cousin Marimo's instructions, I had stood patiently in line and now here I was: a whole college student holding a loaded crate of eggs like Judas Iscariot wondering what to do with his shiny coins. I had played along more from a sense of curiosity than anything else. I had roared with laughter earlier that morning when Marimo announced quite casually that the Party was distributing eggs to its supporters. But how was I supposed to know my cousin would become something of an accidental hero that very afternoon?

In truth I didn't need these eggs at all since, to begin with, I ate at the college's dining hall. Yet I had even hummed along to two or three *chimurenga* songs as the crowd sought to keep up their morale while a few trusted hands unloaded crate upon crate of eggs from a Party truck. Now I felt a sickness just above the navel. I turned round and looked about for some sad-faced child who could really use my eggs. The whole business was funny in a strange way. Whoever had heard of a political party giving out eggs? But in our Zimbabwe, money had become useless – even the fat cats at the Statistics Office had given up trying to calculate the rate of inflation. Listening to my cousin earlier that morning, tears of laughter had rolled down my face when I tried to imagine the exact relationship between a big, smooth egg and the Party, the same outfit that had bossed us around for 28 unbroken years. Like our politics had anything to do with protein levels in ghettoes, where enterprising youths had even turned to stripping and selling the street signs. As I was wrestling with these thoughts, someone accidentally knocked my arm from behind. Before I could move a muscle, the whole tray lay waste at my feet.

"These ones are only slightly cracked, *mwanangu*," said a voice that resembled that of my long-departed mother. "Here, these ones are still good." She crouched at my feet, carefully sorting the usable eggs from the yellow and white mess on the ground. I shook my head and started to walk away, ashamed of the spectacle but happy to be free of the crate. The woman gleefully continued to gather up the half-cracked eggs.

"Hey, Chiko, where are you going?" This was my cousin Marimo, a tight bundle of a man who told everyone I was his brother. Only that morning I had discovered that his fellow Party youths called him Comrade Advance. It was hard to imagine this was my cousin and former classmate who, only a year before, was promising his parents that he would pass his exams, go to college to study medicine and take good care of them in a few years. After the high school examination results were released, Marimo had withdrawn into his shell like a timid tortoise for a while. There was no point asking him if he had passed. When the government issued the one trillion dollar note and the inflation rate galloped into a figure with a dizzying number of zeroes, Marimo had drifted towards the Party's youth movement, muttering darkly about sell-outs and 'our enemies'. Now here he was, walking around with some of his old swagger thanks to the Party, the same party whose ancient leaders told anyone who cared to listen that they had died for the country's freedom even as they stood proselytising. "We now have the land and what we now need are the inputs to start producing," Marimo said one day, showing me his name in the government's newspaper. The government was giving people land, including people like my very own cousin Marimo, who was in fact both a *born-free* and a *born-location* and had never swung a hoe in his life. It was common knowledge that the government usually had nothing but scorn for *born-frees* and *born-locations* like Marimo; after all, they had not died for the country. That aside, if the government's own newspaper was to be believed, my cousin had been allocated land in a place bearing the strange name of Jompani. We had never heard of such a place. I had resisted the temptation to ask him if he thought Jompani was in Zimbabwe at all.

"Have you gone to inspect your land?" I had asked instead, faking a cough to suppress the laughter.

"Not yet, but a friend tells me this Jompani is all bush you know. I wish they had given me a piece of one of these farms we are acquiring from *mabhunu.*"

"But you have to start somewhere, right?" I pressed.

"Yes. But I have heard there are trees that are as fat as drums on some of those uncultivated lands. A Party cadre died recently after chopping down one of those trees with an axe. Anyway, we have received maize seed packs and a bit of fertilizer now," Marimo said, gazing into the distance.

"You have received those?" This was the first time I had heard that my very own relative had actually received farming inputs from the government's much-touted land reform programme that the Party sometimes spoke of as a war.

"Yes. But they only gave us ten bags of maize seed and five bags of fertilizer each," he said.

"That's not bad really. Where are they?" I was curious.

"I sold some, well… most of them in fact… to raise a little cash to go see my new farm. But you know how things are with this dollar these days. Now I will need to raise more funds with this inflation," he said with a shrug. I watched him while he took a pull from his home-made cigarette as if that was raising more funds for a trip to Jompani.

It bothered me that this is what had become of my cousin; part of a human conveyer belt that distributed eggs to the cheerful Party crowd while half-dreaming of the day he would visit this Jompani that was already something of a promised land in his family. But it was a promised land whose allure seemed to partly depend on it being like a mirage in the desert. It was there and yet not there. It was as if its intoxicating aroma tormented and excited my cousin.

What had happened to the idea of going to the city polytechnic to study printing technology? Marimo had talked about that after discovering he didn't qualify for the university. These days he did not even mention it. For a while, it was just the government paper with his name in it that seized his attention. One weekend I visited him from college and I had dutifully stared at the newspaper with my cousin's name in it. Yes, there it was; MARIMO, MARIMO, staring back at me. He was one of those chaps whose last name was identical to the first name.

Oh, how my cousin had changed. Where was the dreamy student of twelve months ago?

"There are positions in the army for the youths if we win this war, this election," he had insisted earlier that morning, already speaking like the old Party men who daily claimed they had died for this country.

"Which war?" I had asked, feigning ignorance.

"What do you think this is? These whites have declared themselves our enemies. We must show them we are now free in this election and kick them out once and for all." At that moment I could have sworn I had heard these same words uttered by the Party boss on television a few days earlier. I had resisted the urge to remind him that the man they were campaigning for in this election had been a Member of Parliament five consecutive times already. That is if one chose to exclude the brief term he had served as a member of the Zimbabwe-Rhodesia regime.

"My crate fell... some woman...," I started.

"Don't worry. I have organized everything."

"Some fool pushed me from behind."

"Shhhh," he said, leaning towards me. He threw his arm around my neck and whispered, "Forget that, brother. Mother has already taken our share home. And some to sell later too!" he added with a wink.

He was talking about his own mother but I let the excitement sweep over my cousin. I did tend to call her mother, as I had lived with the family while at school. I had left before Marimo had graduated from high school to be a half-hearted paper-farmer and now a dodgy street politician for a party that didn't mind dishing out eggs to the residents of this ghetto, where muggers now ambushed their prey from behind mountains of uncollected rubbish. I fingered my own Party membership card, hastily acquired that very morning just for the egg 'donation'. "Those who oppose us will get their eggs from Blair," he had said with a hearty guffaw. "Or Bush," he added, as an afterthought. I had resisted the urge to inform him that both Tony Blair and George Bush had in fact left office a while back.

"So we are done, right?" I asked, doing my best to show how bored I was.

"No, Chiko," he said. Then, pointing with his chin, he added, "That water bowser over there is full of the best 'riversand' in town." I knew 'riversand' meant opaque beer, the kind people like my cousin sometimes drank at sunrise 'just to fix last night's hangover', only to end up getting drunk again and having to repeat the same procedure the next day. The brew was cheap and bought from a tap inside the many thriving beerhalls that now competed with the mushrooming evangelical churches for ghetto residents' attention. I turned to follow the direction of his stretched-out chin. The mid-October sun was now at its fiery peak. What could be better than to walk back to my cousin's parents' house, take a cold shower in the slimy shared bathroom, drink some water and politely excuse myself and escape back to college? Just why did my father insist that I should visit his brother's family at least once a semester? Just because they had housed and fed me for two years of my high school? Clearly we had less and less to talk about these days. Even Marimo wasn't someone I really wanted to spend too much time with anymore.

"Look, Marimo, you know I don't drink."

"Come on, brother. Maybe you now drink white people's stuff... you know, the expensive stuff."

"No. In fact one of the reasons I will never drink is because white people stopped us from brewing our own beer and are now raking in all the profits because of people like you who will not stop to...."

He shrugged his shoulders. "OK, OK, my big brother. You probably have your whisky bottle at college. Here, I have these two empty containers. I will give you one and, if you want, you can donate it to your dear brother." He laughed at his own wit.

"When is this happening? I really must get going. I have school tomorrow."

"But today is only a Saturday."

"I have a prac at the lab," I lied. I knew 'prac' would impress him more than 'practical'.

He eyed me dubiously like an antique dealer eyeing a rusty coin, then said, "OK, let's do this and then we carry the brew straight home. You can go then." He dashed back to his spot in the human conveyer belt.

I looked at the crowd and everyone seemed to be talking – and shouting – all at once. I adjusted my cap and gazed at the crowd through half-closed eyes. As people in the queue appeared to transform into tiny ants with proboscis-like mouths, another of those *chimurenga* songs rose again:

Be a hero, be a hero
Be a hero, be a hero
And defeat the enemy
And defeat the enemy

Heroes who fight over eggs? I turned to spit my disgust into a tuft of grass and saw a multi-coloured chameleon. I held my spit. The song rose, fell, rose, fell with the lead singer throwing the challenge to the rest of the crowd who responded joyously, tossing back the song at the lead singer as crate upon crate changed hands right behind me. The chameleon's blue-green belly rose, fell, rose, fell. As children we were sworn enemies of chameleons, which defiantly copied the colours of our clothes even as we attacked them. We used to believe that a chameleon brought bad luck if it changed its colour to match that of your shirt. This chameleon's round eye seemed to be gazing into my soul. I felt a need to protect it, and was about to find a stick to carry it away from the crowd before some vicious kid stamped on it, when my cousin called out my name. I walked towards Marimo.

He threw two empty 20 litre containers to me and continued shouting along with other Party youths. At the edge of the clearing, others were pinning up posters of their candidate. I asked for one of the posters from a cheerful girl in Party regalia. There he was, the candidate with 'Prof' in front of his name. Although he now wore glasses, he had pushed them to the gleaming tip of his bulb of a nose and he was smiling generously at me from the centre of the poster. Near the top was a smaller picture of the Party president, who seemed unsure whether he should smile or just stare at the camera. The president's picture wasn't a new one. We had seen it everywhere since independence. Then his hair was greying gracefully above his rounded face. These days the hair was black, a black so extreme it shone in the afternoon sun.

"Chiko! Chiko! Bring the first container!" I looked up and there was Marimo, standing precariously on a ladder as he worked to open the lid of the bowser that contained the cheap brew. The song had changed now and the orderliness of the egg queue was gone. I inched forward, battling some sharp male elbows and shrill-voiced women whose mouths watered at the prospect of dipping their beaks in the free brew. At the foot of the ladder, holding it in place, was one Party cadre in an oversized Party T-shirt from a past election campaign, a tiny cigarette smouldering at one corner of his mouth. I shoved some more and pushed my container towards my cousin who skillfully used his big toe to hook it by the handle.

I spread my legs, defending my position from the surging crowd. I waited for Marimo to lower the first full container. One of the women was singing right into my ear. Like most of the women, she was dressed in the colourful Party T-shirt that bore a younger image of the Party leader. What made these women grow so fat even in these thin years? I looked up and saw only my cousin's bare feet as he reached down into the belly of the bowser. Then time stood still. A surge in the crowd caught me completely by surprise. The over-sized Party woman fell into me, knocking me sideways. The Party youth at the foot of the ladder cursed as he was trampled by maddened feet. After what seemed like hours, I emerged at one end of the crowd, bruised, dazed and limping. Everyone was pointing at the open top of the bowser, yelling and screaming.

Only then did I realise my cousin had fallen into the belly of the bowser. The ladder had broken in two as people fell in the stampede and now the Party cadres were throwing their hands about helplessly. Women scurried away from the bowser in terror. I hobbled wildly into the midday sun.

The following morning, Marimo's younger brother found me lying face up in a college hospital bed. From the corner of my eye, I saw him shuffle hesitantly towards the bed. A nurse showed him to an empty chair near my bed. I considered feigning sleep but the boy had already seen me as he entered.

"He's quite unstable so be careful what you tell him," the nurse said and walked to another bed. My younger cousin sat down, thrust his hands between his thighs and waited. I ignored him and soon I was looking at a praying mantis that appeared at the window sill.

"People are going to the Goats' Place this afternoon," he said a few moments after I had ignored his tentative greeting. "The Party is paying for everything. The Party branch declared him a silver heart hero for dying while serving the people. They said we should come back together quickly." I didn't move. He sat for a while and then said he was leaving.

"I lost my cousin a long time ago," I shouted at the retreating boy and was surprised by my anger. I turned to my praying mantis. I drifted into sleep.

I woke up to my father's angry voice. "Are you not a man? Is this how you will behave when you marry and become a father?" He was sitting in the chair vacated by my cousin two hours earlier. I had learnt a long time ago not to respond when he was like this. Eventually I was discharged and I left the hospital with my father, as he continued to insist that I should have been more of a man. The nurse had given me a wooden stick to use as a walking aid.

"I drove from Kwekwe last night when I heard about the loss. I came with your mother," my father said as we shuffled along. Even after all these years I had little to say to my step-mother, let alone think of her as mother. The old man knew this so he sometimes volunteered information about her, since I never asked.

"You are now a man," my father said, as if I needed reminding every five minutes.

"My breath is quite short," I said, lest he forgot the nurse's words of just a few minutes ago. I held on to his shoulder and walked with an exaggerated limp. Sweat poured down his neck into his white shirt. A true product of British colonial culture, he was turned out in a black suit, necktie and felt hat. It bothered me that we had never been friends enough for me to tease him about such things. Almost as tall as me, he laboured as he dragged me up the small hill towards the parking lot where his tiny red Mini Cooper stood, ageless as ever. I was relieved to discover my step-mother wasn't in the car.

"Your mother is helping at the funeral," he said.

I flopped in and watched him go through the familiar rituals of starting the ancient car. The old thing wheezed and moaned in protest but father was determined. The car eventually groaned to life and we crawled out of the college grounds. Some old Catholic hymn was playing on his radio. Hadn't this man heard of the *Vapostori* choral songs that even drunkards were singing in the beer gardens these days? We eased into the city centre heading in the direction of the Goats' Place, the big cemetery where the city people buried their dead.

Twice the old man tried to get me to talk about cousin Marimo's accident, but I remained quiet, looking at Harare's overflowing streets. At the robots a little boy sucking on a tube of glue stretched a grey hand towards me. I refused to meet his gaze. We stopped for the old man to buy some fast food. I sat back and watched two small girls in heavy make-up chat animatedly with a much older, colourfully-dressed man. What sort of man dresses in cuff-links in this weather? A large banner above the trio's heads read: 'Archipelago Nitespot'.

Just as the old man returned, police sirens cut through the afternoon air. My father held onto the Mini Cooper's half-open door. Only two police cars drove past and I realised it wasn't the president's motorcade as I had initially thought. I craned my neck to get a better view. Behind the police vehicles was a hearse and then two more police cars. Behind these was a huge open truck, the kind that touts called the frying pan. It was packed with chanting youths who waved brightly-coloured flags and newly-printed placards. As the truck came up opposite us, I looked at one of the signs, which was dominated by a photograph of Marimo. Below his smiling face, he was described by the epitaph: 'MARIMO MARIMO: HERO OF THE PIOPLE'. Scores of youths ran alongside the truck, swinging the Party flags and posters this way and that while chanting my cousin's name.

I eased out of the car and looked at the old man, who remained standing as if frozen by his side of the car. He stood silently as three more trucks filed past in the direction of the cemetery. I started walking away, laughing hysterically.

"What is it?" I heard my father ask.

"I am going back to college," I said, without breaking my stride. "Let them bury their hero," I shouted and, with that, threw away the walking stick. I wasn't shuffling now.

Sudden Death

Blessing Musariri

The rain here knows nothing of seasons. It is not looked for on horizons like rain back home, where it is always imminent, predicted, but falls unexpectedly. I long for the sun.

I am Agnes here. No one looks at the picture closely. No one questions why sometimes there is another Agnes who comes in who looks nothing like the Agnes they already know. Not often, but I would have thought that by now someone would have smelt a rat. No. It's just, "Oh hello Agnes, you've changed your hair again today. I liked it better yesterday."

"Oh hello Agnes, Bertie's had an accident, will you be a dear and change him?"

"Oh Agnes, there you are!" Oh help me God. I long for hot, red earth under my bare feet and for no one to say the name Agnes in my presence.

It's been two weeks and I still feel as if I'm floating – hovering above the surface, making no real contact with anyone, untouched by anything. In this in-between place it doesn't matter if you get up in the morning or if you don't. It doesn't matter if you speak to no one all day, if no one touches you, if no one sees you. It doesn't matter if you live or die. It rains all the time and the world is a hazy mist beyond which the sound of traffic blares undistracted. Where people brush past each other impatiently in the streets and greet you with well practised cheer in shops and over the phone.

"Oh Agnes! It's lovely to have you back. So sorry about your loss."

"Agnesh dear, you are sho tanned, did you have a lovely holiday?"

Olive is oblivious. She has taken out her teeth again and now I will spend all morning hunting for them. She wants me to comb the memory of hair that remains on her smooth liver-spotted scalp. I have often wondered why there is so little of it left. It's not common for women to lose all their hair like this – even at such an advanced age.

Gloria didn't want to get up this morning. It's her daily routine – not wanting to get up but getting up anyway. I know how she feels. Yesterday when I shook her awake she looked clear into my eyes and said, "Am I in Africa dear? When did we get here?" She travelled a lot in her youth in the forties and sometimes tells me about her experiences with 'friendly natives'. The natives here are friendly too.

Sylvia is cheerful when I walk into her room. She used to be a dancer She has the body of a small well-proportioned doll but when she is angry and moody, her strength is that of a strong young man. She bites, she kicks, she slaps. I don't know what gets into her. She is pinning her pristine white bun on the top of her head – there is not one hair out of place.

"Oh Agnes, I did miss you. I had such a cramp in my legs yesterday and you're the only one who knows how to take it away. You are back now and it's all just dandy."

"You look nice dear." It's Arnold. He was a plumber for forty-three years. Sometimes I find him walking around with a wrench in his hand or any other tool he manages to find. We have to be very careful what is left in accessible areas – they would hate to be sued by distressed relatives should an accident occur. The other day he had a mop.

"Oh there you are Agnes. Don't worry, I'll mop that spill right up. You shouldn't have any more problems with that sink now." Arnold is gentle and kind even when he is moving around in the confusion of his past life. Today as he comes up to me he takes my hand in both of his and says:

"Agnes dear, no one can ever say anything to make the loss of a loved one easier. My wife died ten years ago and sometimes it feels like it was just yesterday. It will take time. You never forget but it gets easier to remember." He smiled at me and for a moment I thought I felt the sun. I wanted to smile back at him but instead I begin to cry.

*

We were sending money back home to build a house and setting some aside for our wedding. We were never meant to have stayed this long. It was just going to be six months. We figured if we both worked double shifts for six months we would make the money we needed but we agreed that, regardless, we would return. England was all very well but the sun only came out for three months of the year and even then, it wasn't guaranteed. We liked the lazy sunshiny life back home, the undemanding pace where even if you were a workaholic, you still couldn't quite avoid having time left over to see friends and family – town closed by lunchtime on Saturdays and only supermarkets opened on Sundays, what choice did you have? I liked it that way.

"What is the purpose of your visit?"
"Where will you be residing?"
"Who is this person to you?"
"How long are you intending to stay?"
"Do you intend to seek employment whilst you are here?"
I forced a calmness I didn't feel and smiled at the colourless woman in front of me. With no change in her expression she stamped six months in my passport.
Simba, two counters down walked through to the luggage carousels. I heaved a sigh of relief. We had decided to separate for the purposes of best chance. Both of us managed to give the right answers, even if very little of what we said was true.

We laughed as we stood at the luggage carousel. Simba was explaining to me that his name was actually an alias. "Look!" he showed me his passport and rummaged in his wallet for his metal ID. "See. Nowhere does it say Simba, just Tonderai Mugarisani Macheka.
"My aunt chose the name but my parents didn't agree. However, it is a testament to my aunt's dint of will that everyone knows me as Simba. How it prevailed above all the others, I will never really know." He shook his head and I marvelled at him – his use of words. Simba used words in speech that the rest of us only read in books, we tend to leave them there.

My cousin Agnes happily gave me her identification. Her husband was an accountant with a good job and all his papers in order; she could afford to stay home with the kids. She worked only occasionally when she felt like getting out of the house.
"Carework or nursing is the best. It's flexible and the money is good

but I won't lie to you – it's not easy."

When I expressed unease at assuming her identity she merely scoffed.

"Ha! Amainini, they will never know the difference, they think all us black people look alike. The darker you are, the more confused they get." It was difficult to believe I would get away with it but it turned out to be true. Things don't have to make sense for them to be true.

*

Arnold is now standing outside bewildered with a broom handle in his hands. I wonder who let him out. He'll catch his death out there. I should call him in but right then I see my father standing tall in his field watching the golden blush of sunrise on the horizon. The maize is up to his thighs and it is lush and green. He laughs at me as I wade through stalks almost as tall as I am and wipes the drops of dew off my cheeks.

"Rosanna, have you ever seen a more beautiful thing?"

I wrap my arm around his middle and feel the warmth of his strong body seeping into mine. I shake my head, feeling a huge bubble of joy unfurling inside me and I hold him tighter.

"It looks like gold, Baba," I say, proud of my inspiration, "it's like we are rich."

Babette rescues Arnold and I'm left staring at the empty patch of garden, burnt by frost.

It's a thirty minute bus ride to the home. We are living with my sister Annette. She's a London veteran of five years and, even thought she's lived in the south-west all her time, she decided on what I have discovered to be a typically East End accent. Annette was smart to come to London when she did, she was able to register and train as a nurse before there was a glut in the system. She earns good money but seems to have no ambition to save it for anything.

"Ain't going back 'ome innit, so I can just enjoy mi loife. I'm still young."

When she goes out with her friends, she slicks her hair right back, so that it looks like it might just slip off her scalp and slide down onto her neck, fastens large gold hoops to her ears, slips on four inch heels and pretends she's a Jamaican 'rude-gyal'. One day Simba told her that she would catch a cold down there, pointing to her barely concealed crotch. She flipped him off with her middle finger and he laughed out loud. He finds her endlessly amusing, but that was the last time I heard an honest laugh from him.

Simba lost both his parents in a bus accident when he was ten. He was shuffled around relatives until he ended up at a mission school with his uncle who was a headmaster there. It was the best time of his life, he tells me. His uncle was resident at the school so Simba was at school all year round. He didn't mind this, he said, he spent all his time in the library and, during the term, it was his proud duty to help with library duties. He has been drifting since leaving school five years ago, looking for a safe place to harbour. He says he has found it in me. This is the beauty of Simba, he has had so little in his life that anything more than he is used to is wealth.

I suppose we are not so different, him and I. We are both without our parents. The day of the riches in the field is my last memory of being with my father. He died soon after, during a time that is hazy in my mind. My mother did not feel obligated to live for much longer after his passing, not even for our sakes and so we were inherited by my aunt – my father's sister. Who is it who sings 'a house is not a home'? Do they continue to say that a house is not a home unless you are there? I don't quite remember the words but I think that is the meaning behind the song. I would say that a house is not a home unless it belongs to you. Simba and I agree. We are tired of calling in at different ports, pretending that we are home. Even Annette's is not home. It's a place to stop for now, on the way to our destination.

*

Everyone said to us there was no point in coming back home, at least not yet – things had gone from bad to worse. We were sending the money to my brother and he was running around buying bricks and cement, finding a crew to start laying down the foundation and just generally making sure that by the time we returned there would be something to show for all our efforts. Simba argued against overstaying, he didn't like things that weren't straightforward.

"It's bad enough we're having to remember to be other people when we go to work, but we never see each other and the jobs themselves are demeaning. I'm a teacher, a good one, and you, an agro-economist in this concrete village. We were never going to stay – remember? Let's just go home and deal with what's there. Others are doing it." He complained that he was sick and tired of mopping up vomit – he worked in a home for alcoholics, "It's not like they're being treated or anything. They are just there so they're not out on the streets. Can you imagine, being so pampered!" he raved. But he didn't have time enough to complete the cycle of his frustration, it was time

128

to leave for his second job stacking shelves in a supermarket. When things were good at the agency, I worked a night shift in the hospital, ten minutes walk from our flat. It was a tough shift, dirty work, but whenever I felt like quitting, I thought of the pleasure of returning to a house that would belong to myself and my husband. There was no way I was going to live with his relatives in their family home. If there was one thing I knew without having to be told, it's that there is no house big enough for two women to run.

We had two months left on our visitor visas and the next time we met in between shifts, we agreed that we were going to press on, but from now on, we would go full out and work as much as we could. Annette generously offered to make up a third of what we were aiming for.

"It's only money innit? I will make it back easy enough."

It seemed like a good plan, and so all we knew of each other in the next few weeks was the various signs of our passing through the flat in between each other's comings and goings: wet towels in the bathroom; unwashed dishes in the sink; a note on the fridge to buy sugar, milk or bread; traces of Annette's perfume in the air; the red dot on the VCR that indicates recording in progress – this is Simba I know, he doesn't like to miss *The Weakest Link*, but there is a growing stack of unwatched tapes in the bookshelf. Time has caught us in a worm-hole and we are hurtling around, each one in their capsule moving relentlessly from one stop to the next. I am Agnes at the home and at the hospital at night. At home there is never anyone to speak my name anymore. I take to saying my name out loud in the bathroom when I look in the mirror but I resemble no one I know and it doesn't stick.

I say my name now, standing at the sink in the kitchen at the home, but it is barely a whisper.

"Agnes, be a love and clean up the mess Sebastian made in the hall. Tiffany's busy upstairs and I can't find Mercy anywhere." I am startled by the intrusion and I wonder how long I have been standing there staring out of the window. Babette is carrying a pile of laundry to the washing machines in the basement. Sebastian is tall and fragile looking. His eyes lie deep in wrinkled sockets and he moves around the house only a little quicker than a sloth. He is often an immobile post smack-dab in the middle of corridors. It's almost like, from one moment to the next, he forgets where it is he meant to go and how it is he means to get there.

"Come along Sebastian." I pull him gently away from the spot where a yellowish puddle has gathered at his feet.

"Let's get you cleaned up." I try to lift my voice in imitation of good cheer but today the same spirit that is slowly dying in Sebastian has found a home in my body, it is taking everything I have in reserve to keep moving.

*

Anne Robinson would most likely swing her fancy lectern around and ask, "What 'c' is a, usually surprising, instance of similar events or circumstances happening at the same time by chance?"

I would not fumble at this answer on this day. It has just so happened that we were all at the flat at the same time, for the first time in about a month and a half; I was not given a hospital shift, Simba had a cold and was too unwell to go into work; Annette, nursing a broken heart, was locked up in her room going over events with one of her friends on the phone. Simba, however, was lying on the couch watching a marathon of *The Weakest Link*, his head on my lap and I was happy to sit with him and let his enthusiasm wash gently over me. He knew many of the answers but he is weakest when it comes to questions on UK geography.

"I would probably get voted off by the other contestants in a conspiracy because I would be one of the stronger players," he stated.

"But if you are the strongest link most of the time you are bound to survive," I assured him.

"Doesn't always work that way, Babes, sometimes they can do some arbitrary thing and, before you know it, you're taking the walk of shame."

I rubbed his head affectionately and leaned down to kiss him.

"Not my baby," I said, suddenly overwhelmed by the warmest feeling inside. I wanted to bundle Simba up in my arms and hold onto him so tight that, when I let go, he would be imprinted on me. It was almost as if, for a moment, the sun was shining on me again, not the weak English winter sun, but the hot yellow sun of back home. Somewhere in the memory of my nostrils I smelt a faint hint of sun-dried sweat and it had never smelt so sweet. I imagined that Simba and I were sitting like this in our own living room, in our own house. Timmy had been sending photos and we were now at window level.

The two contestants left on the show were going into 'sudden death'. Simba reached up and twined his fingers with mine, smiling in anticipation. In this moment, I knew it for the truth it was, we were both happy.

Annette called from her bedroom to pick up the extension in the living room.

"It's Aunty Saru," she yelled. "She wants to speak to you."

It was winter again, without warning. It was as if someone had opened up a window and let in the February frost. It felt like bad news and I had not even picked up the phone. I knew this simply because this is what follows a moment of imagined sunshine in the dead of winter, when it's too late at night for even the mind's tricks.

"Hello," I said with trepidation.

It didn't really sink in when she said it. The story is so round-about and complicated. Even though it hadn't all sunk in, I'd heard enough to cause my brain to stop processing any further than what was salient. Silently I put the receiver to Simba's ear, I could not trust that I would be able to recount what I thought I had just been told. He had to hear it for himself and tell it to me again. Simba is never at a loss for words, he uses words that some of us left behind at school, small words that nobody notices, big ones that no one can spell and middle-sized words that mean exactly what they sound like. But Simba placed the receiver back in its cradle and said nothing. I saw him wilting in front of my eyes, the breath simply left his body and did not seem to return so that he folded over like a plucked leaf in the sun without recourse to water. He rubbed his hands over his face but the tiredness remained etched in the grooves. He was as bewildered as I was suddenly hollow.

*

Sebastian is cleaned up and ensconced in an armchair near the fire. The hall is mopped up and restored. Sylvie is twirling dreamily on the rug in the centre of the living room. Her arm is bent gracefully above her head, which she has thrown back, eyes closed. She will probably become dizzy but I let her continue. Olive's teeth are on the coffee table next to her seat and she is gumming a biscuit. She will be fine, it's only a biscuit. It will eventually become a soggy mess. Gloria is staring out of the window twisting a pristine handkerchief around her fingers – she is most likely reliving her adventurous past. Arnold lumbers by, surprisingly unencumbered. He reaches out to squeeze my arm and he winks. I am tired. The tiredness will not leave me. I told them that I had had some bad news from home. They have all been very kind and supportive, thinking I had lost a loved one. How can I explain the sudden death of the dream that Simba and I have shared over the past five months. The evaporation of the reason I have come here day in and out, smiling and being friendly and helpful when I would rather have been standing in the middle of a field sweltering in gum-boots and sheltering under a cotton bush-hat talking about rain that is yet to come – looking for it on the horizon, praying that it would not abuse us this year.

*

"So we have spent five months of our lives in service to her majesty's citizens out of the goodness of our hearts!"

"At the airport when the immigration official asked, we should have just said, 'no, we are here as volunteers'."

When he recovered from the shock, Simba threw the remote control at the wall and started to pace angrily about the room, occasionally sweeping things off surfaces and onto the floor. I sat quiet and unmoving where he had left me on the sofa.

"Wot's his problem then?" Annette asked from the doorway to her room.

"Your bloody brother!" Simba pointed an accusing finger at Annette but she was unmoved, 'rude-gyal' that she is.

"Yeah? Wot's he gone and done?"

Simba could not speak the words. He turned away harshly and marched into our room. Annette came to sit beside me.

"Go on then, wot's he gone and done?"

"He's been sending us photos of someone else's building. He hasn't bought anything with our money – no cement, no bricks, no one's been hired to do anything, there's nothing." My voice was dull, my words matter-of-fact. I wasn't sure if what I was saying was the truth, it was simply what I knew then.

"WOT! Timmy! That wanker! Wot's 'e playin' at?" Annette reached over for the phone.

"He's been missing for a week, turns out he's in South Africa."

"We should never have trusted him, the little cunt. How could he do such a thing?" In her outrage, Annette moved away from the East End by degrees until she was the Annette I knew when she first left, and for the smallest second it felt like coming home – a brief comfort.

We have to decide whether to stay and start again or simply face the loss and return home. Timmy is the weakest link and we are the two left standing; the next step we take will make or break us. Simba doesn't like things that are not straightforward; he will be suspended in anger for some time. All I can think of is that I am longing for the sun.

Tomato Stakes

John Eppel

Catha edulis or Bushman's tea, as it is known locally, possesses nothing like the stimulation of its northern relative, khat. Nevertheless, when the young leaves and shoots are infused in boiling water, it makes a refreshing drink. The Ndebele people do not call it *inandinandi* for nothing. When Lofty Pienaar was driven off his Umgusa farm by the Deputy Director of Youth Brigades (who graciously let him keep his house and 10 hectares of land) he made a decision, after consulting his foreman of 20 years, Tobias Banda, to go into commercial production of this small indigenous tree.

Lofty Pienaar had been at boarding school with me in the 60s. His father worked at the Beta asbestos mine just outside Gwanda. My father worked at the Lannenhurst asbestos mine just outside West Nicholson. So we had something in common – fathers who would probably die of asbestosis. On our way to and from school, we shared a compartment (with other boarders) in the steam train that huffed and puffed between Bulawayo and the South-Western districts, and we shared a fascination for the bush. Every Sunday, after church, we would bunk out of the hostel and head for the little patch of wilderness that flourished between our school and the race course. There we would trap mice, shoot small creatures (with our catapults), and raid birds' nests for our burgeoning egg collection. The mice we would skin, hoarding the pelts until we had enough – hundreds – to make a *kaross*. We used coarse salt to preserve the tiny pelts and to flavour the birds, usually *mossies*, which we sometimes managed to shoot, then pluck, gut, and cook over surreptitious fires.

Once, I spent a school holiday with Lofty, and once, he spent a school holiday with me. The Pienaars – Mom, Dad, little Johann, and Lofty – lived

133

in an unusual house. It consisted of one very large room partitioned by curtains into three smaller rooms: a bedroom for the parents, a bedroom for the boys, and a living-cum-dining room. The kitchen and 'bathroom' were in a separate construction a few metres away from the house. Now this house had walls made of burlap coal bags, which had been sewn together with tying wire. These had then been nailed to creosote-treated blue gum poles and then painted, over and over, with whitewash. Lofty couldn't wait for a windy day to show me how their house actually flapped. The roof was thatch supported by chicken wire and slender blue gum poles.

When the Pienaars first moved into the house there had been no running water, so Lofty's dad got permission to lay a pipe from the asbestos workings down to the kitchen building, a square *pondok* with a tin roof. Then he built a chip geyser, and next to it a not very private shower, which was sometimes like Father Bear's porridge – too hot, sometimes like Mother Bear's porridge – too cold, and never like Baby Bear's porridge – just right.

Their toilet was a long drop quite a distance from the house, and quite a scary place to visit by night because of snakes, scorpions and centipedes. It was also quite a scary place to visit by day because of itinerant cows who liked to munch on the half-hearted grass screen that surrounded the thunder-box.

We had fun those holidays. I especially enjoyed our forays into the bush, sparse because of the white, alkaline sub-soil, but made magical by the clonk of donkey bells and the sudden sweet scent of wild gardenia.

We had as much fun at our house, which was situated on a hill outside West Nicholson. We had no running water but there was a concrete reservoir almost as big as the house, which caught the rain. We spent hours every day playing in this algae infested frogs' paradise. That was where my sister and I had learned to swim, and that was the water my mother used for her vegetable garden. I showed Lofty the prim rows of tomato stakes, *kanniedood* switches, which had taken root and were growing into saplings. It looked like a miniature plantation. My mother had to keep trimming them back so that they would not smother the tomatoes. One morning Lofty and I helped her pollinate the tomato flowers with pollen from pawpaw flowers. My mother believed that this would produce larger and juicier fruits, and indeed, her tomatoes – a type called 'ox heart' – were magnificent specimens.

Water for the household was brought every evening by the mine lorry. It was decanted from a 40 gallon drum into various containers, the largest being a zinc bath. Normally my father bathed first, and since he was always filthy from his long hard days at the mine, he would leave quite a scum behind him on the surface of the water. Then it was my mother's turn, then my sister's, then mine. Since Lofty was our guest, he got to bath first, in the clean water.

Our house didn't flap like the Pienaars, but it creaked. It was brick under iron and consisted of three rooms and a verandah. Lofty and I slept on the verandah. We kept the mosquitoes away by burning citronella oil. We were somewhat alarmed by the vesper bats which flitted in and out, because, the term before, our English teacher had been reading extracts to us from Bram Stoker's book on Count Dracula. We made ourselves necklaces of garlic, and we carved wooden stakes, which we kept under our pillows. My sister refused to lend us her silver crucifix, but we produced makeshift crosses with combinations of cutlery.

The road up to our house was steep, ideal for the go-carts Lofty and I made those holidays, out of discarded tricycle and pram wheels. My mother sewed us a chequered flag from bits of old underwear, and my sister (who had been growing more and more interested in Lofty) kept us supplied with Kipto, a cheap, orange-flavoured concentrate of the time, and cocoa powder mixed with sugar.

On one occasion we went to a dinner-dance at the Colleen Bawn club where we met up with hostel friends like Fred Simpson and Andy Visagie. We spent hours playing on the trampoline down at the swimming pool, and later, we went fruit stealing in the Phillips's garden. We chose the Phillips's for two reasons: their dogs were friendly, and they grew Hanepoot and Catawba grapes. Who wants to steal prickly pears and guavas when you can get grapes? Unfortunately, we had overlooked the fact that Phineas, the Phillips's old Malawian cook, was a light sleeper on account of being terrified of unsolicited visits by nocturnal *tokoloshes*. Our shirts were crammed with bunches of grapes when he emerged from his *khaya* brandishing a *knobkerrie*. Fred and Andy ran in one direction, and Lofty and I ran in another, offloading our loot along the way. The old man chased us screaming *"Tsotsis! Tsotsis!"*

"Tina haikona choncha! Tina haikona choncha!" Lofty screamed in terrified reply. Phineas would have caught us if he hadn't been so old, and beaten the living daylights out of us. Those were good times. Lofty and my sister, Lisa, became sweethearts thereafter, and they were together for several years. They finally broke up because my sister decided to become a born again Christian awash with the blood of Christ, while Lofty stuck to his Dutch Reformed roots.

After school we went our different ways, I into social work, Lofty into farming. He had been trained at Gwebi Agricultural College near Harare, and he was working as an assistant foreman on a tobacco farm somewhere in Mashonaland when he was called up, as I was, and all white men between the ages of 18 and 60, to help keep the Rhodesian Front in power. The next time I met him was at Vila Salazar on the Mozambique border. It turned out that we had both been posted to Sixth Battalion as B grade riflemen, which meant, mostly, digging bunkers and pit latrines. It was during an ambush deep in the Gonarezhou Game Reserve, before we were ordered to "Shut the fuck up", that Lofty confided to me his dream of one day farming his own land.

That day came, ironically, after Independence. The sudden departure of thousands of white people, including landowners, meant that certain farms could be purchased for a song. With help from his parents and his brother, then living in the U.S.A., Lofty put down the deposit on 350 hectares of prime land on the Umgusa River, near enough to Bulawayo for a market gardening project. A condition of his purchase was that he kept on the existing workforce of twenty men and women who lived with their families in a compound on the farm. The head of this workforce was an elderly master farmer called Tobias Banda, respectfully known to all as *Baba*, or Father.

As soon as he received his letter of No Interest from the new government, Lofty, with the help of his loyal workforce, set about transforming what amounted to not much more than a weekend family getaway (the previous owner had been a doctor with a practice in town) into a highly productive industry. In no time he began to supply Bulawayo, and then the entire country, with rich thick cream from his small herd of Jersey cows, the finest wool from his Angora rabbits, and, from his irrigated market garden, artichokes, garlic, lettuce, potatoes, pimentos, and bean sprouts. He also became a major supplier of honey, and jellies made from wild fruits such as marula, kei apple and *uzagogwane*. When he started producing saffron from the dried stigmas of *Crocus sativus*, Lofty entered the world market.

As the years passed, Lofty Pienaar metamorphosed into a wealthy commercial farmer with all the trappings which that status insisted upon: a Mercedes Benz, a house boat on Kariba, a wife and four children, and a place on the Board of at least one private school. Once a year, usually during the Easter Break, we would get together – biltong and beer – and reminisce about the bad old days. Then the farm invasions began, the so-called Third *Chimurenga*. The first invaders were disgruntled war veterans and unemployed youths. They terrorised Lofty's workers by calling them *mtengesi*, and threatening to cut their throats. They were often drunk or high on *mbanje*; they carried axes and *knobkerries*; they banged tin cans and dustbin lids, shouted slogans, and sang songs of liberation.

By the time the second invaders arrived Lofty's workforce had been reduced to one, the elderly Tobias Banda. The compound had been burned to the ground, families dumped on the verges of the road to Victoria Falls. The second wave of invaders were rifle wielding policemen hired by the Deputy Director of Youth Brigades, who accompanied them waving a letter from someone very high up in the Ministry of Agriculture. This letter gave him the right to take over Lofty's farm. The Pienaars were given 24 hours to vacate the property or suffer arrest and imprisonment. But when the Deputy Director of Youth Brigades, after a cursory tour, decided that there were not sufficient power points in the house to service his daughters' computers, his son's play station, and his wife's DVD, not to mention the other three television sets, he graciously allowed Lofty to keep the house – for the time being – as well as surrounding land amounting to 10 hectares or so.

The original invaders, who had transformed Lofty's market garden into a failed mealie field (someone had stolen the irrigation pump), but who were making quite a good living selling firewood and bush meat, at first welcomed the arrival of the police believing that they were there on behalf of them. Up until then, Lofty had managed to appease the ex-combatants (a number of whom would have been mere twinkles in their mothers' eyes on Independence Day) by giving them a Jersey cow to eat once a month. Their smoke-stained eyeballs widened in shock and indignation when the policemen's rifle barrels swivelled away from the Pienaar family and rested on them. They were ordered to vacate the farm immediately. Several shots were fired into the air to show that the Deputy Director meant business. Such are the vicissitudes of living history.

The leaves and bark of *Catha edulis* contain chemicals, which have a stimulating effect on the nervous system, similar to amphetamines, but the Voortrekkers, and long before them the aboriginal peoples of SouthernAfrica, used them as a treatment for chest complaints and influenza. All four of Lofty's children had suffered from croup, and it was Tobias Banda who had brought them relief by making them inhale the steam from boiling fresh *inandinandi* leaves. The old man knew where to find the small, evergreen trees with their drooping branches and pretty, serrated leaves. He and Lofty scoured *Brachystegia* woods and rocky hillsides in the communal lands surrounding Bulawayo district; and they collected seeds by the thousand, which they planted and germinated in individual black plastic bags. Lofty did some research, and calculated that they would reap their first crop of leaves after seven or eight years of growth. Meanwhile he sold his assets, piecemeal, to keep food on the table and his children at school.

Five years later, Lofty's first batch of trees was looking good. Their pale grey, slender trunks were straight and true, their shimmering canopies already resembling the Australian blue gum. He and Tobias had built a leaf-curing barn similar to the ones Lofty had worked with in his tobacco farming days. Their plan was to market a dry product as well as fresh leaves for immediate consumption. Meanwhile, the Deputy Director's 340 hectares had become completely deforested. From horizon to horizon not a single tree, not a single shrub, could be seen. It had all gone into firewood. Time for another cash crop. Tomatoes. Why not? But tomatoes need stakes, and the only stakes left on the Deputy Director's farm were the two that held up his washing line. He called in his erstwhile tree fellers and, looking meaningfully at Lofty's property, offered them 5 cents for every stake that they delivered to his door. A few hours later he found himself happily possessed of 1000 tomato stakes, and Lofty Pienaar was ruined.

The day he hanged himself, from the lintel above the front door of his house, was the same day that Tobias Banda was found murdered in his hut, the word BLANTYRE carved on his chest. The war veterans were back, reinforced by army deserters, some waving AK-47s, others fondling hand grenades with rusty pins. In their wake, in permanent second gear, growled a silver Toyota Land Cruiser Prado VX Turbo Diesel 4x4 with bull bars, and all the mod cons including mp3, electric windows, air bags, and a place to hold a can of coke. (The driver cannot be named but I can tell you that she inhabits the very largest 'small house' in Bulawayo, a pseudo-Tuscan style mansion boasting no fewer than 30 en-suite bedrooms. I can also tell you that she flies to Dubai once a month to shop for clothes, handbags, shoes, and Kentucky fried chicken with chips and tomato sauce.)

She had hired the *toyi-toying* mob in front of her to evict the Deputy Minister of Youth Brigades from his farm. The podgy fingers of her bangled arm were waving a letter with a stamp from the office of the most powerful ministry in the land. She wanted this farm for her younger sister. She had already provided for her two brothers, all her surviving uncles and aunts, and both her unofficial lovers. One way or the other, she owned – for the time being – half of Matabeleland, nearly all of it deforested.

What happened to Lofty's family? They moved in with me. We are in the long and tedious process of emigrating to New Zealand where social workers are in short supply. Pam is a state registered nurse so she won't have any trouble getting employment. Lofty's blatant suicide and the grisly murder of Tobias have severely traumatized all of the children, especially little Theuns, the *laat lammetjie*. They have been going to counselling with a highly regarded NGO organization. Time will tell. Me, I have mixed feelings about leaving the land of my birth. I am a fourth generation European-African. Lofty was a three hundred and fifty-year European-African. So what! We plan to scatter his ashes on a windy day, one that would have made his family's Beta Mine house flap.

The Need

Sandisile Tshuma

"Out of suffering have emerged the strongest souls; the most massive characters are seared with scars." – Kahlil Gibran

Worlds beyond worlds. In all my thirty one years I have never laid eyes on such a beautiful woman. She is coffee with lots of cream in it. A cappuccino my eyes drink in disbelief. She has thick ringlets of jet black hair pulled back at the front and reaching out riotously to the sky from behind. In her eyes are deep, dark pools of mystery and allure that take me places I have never been before, worlds beyond worlds. She is smiling at me and saying something but I do not respond because I am falling into the windows of her soul and my mind is paralysed with awe. That's when you step in, ever the ladies' man, and tell her it's such a coincidence because we're going to Germiston too. Does she work there? No, she doesn't, but she has an interview at nine so if all goes well maybe we'll all be commuting to Germiston together in the future. You assure her that no one in their right mind would deny her a job because of her incredible er, erm… intelligence. She smiles. Stunning.

    The two of you continue talking while I sit wordlessly between you, transfixed by those eyes and desperately willing the frog in my throat to go back from where it came. You're from Mamelodi and she is from Eritrea. Eyes briefly downcast. But she's staying with her brother in Bruma, she quickly adds, noticing the flicker of your eye and the sudden shift in the attention of the other passengers in the minibus from admiration to something colder. In all this time her eyes have not left me. I am suddenly overcome with the need to reassure her that it's fine, that she is not alone and not to worry, I am a foreigner too. Ever the bumbling fool I launch into a hopeless spiel about how it's good to come across a fellow *kwerekwere* and isn't it great how we're practically taking over this country and soon there will be more foreigners than South Africans in Johannesburg. I laugh a little too loudly and turn to face you for reassurance, only to be met by a look that makes my blood run cold. Clearly, I have crossed a line. *Nxa!* I hear a voice behind me, *lomuntu uyasinyatsa.* You are furious and I conclude that this is probably how it comes to pass. Rumours of foreign nationals brutally attacked by mobs of locals in the townships or farms around South Africa have been doing the rounds lately. Although you and I are friends, I know that I have provoked you; you are a hard man and, like many, you live with a life-long fury simmering just beneath the surface. You are not one to be provoked. I know you well enough to know that, in the world you inhabit, pride and masculinity are commonly expressed with a show of violence and taking a life is not a concept that scares you. The minibus is so quiet I can hear myself inhaling and exhaling and it is suddenly incredibly cold. You know this story. You saw it two years ago.

I do not want to die and so if you do this I will run. Through the grimy, untarred sewage strewn streets of this township, past runny-nosed, barefoot children too young to see the sky turn black, I will run.And as you chase after me chanting words full of poison, hate and ugliness, I the *kwerekwere*, the insufferable brother born to another mother, will run from the shack I call home that you in your rage will have set ablaze. Then, as Thabo, John, Tshepo and Mandla join in the senseless chase, I will falter for just a moment, stunned at the vicious treachery of people who have lived with me as friends, not just neighbours. But what is this? What does it mean? Does it mean nothing to you that I have been here at your side day after day, queuing at the taxi rank, drinking at our secret spot and debating if 'Amakhosi' or 'Ama-Buccaneer' will win the Soweto derby this football season? As my feet pound on the dirt my eyes will see not the way ahead of me, but fleeting images of walking this very route just yesterday with you and you and you, tired after a long day at work in the city that promised us gold but has eaten our souls instead.

Tearing past Aus' Lulu's spaza shop, where I bought matches to light my paraffin lamp just the other day, I will hope briefly for this warmhearted woman to offer me protection and talk you out of your insanity. She's got spirit this Lulu. Everyone admires her and looks to her as the iconic strong African woman. For years she endured alcohol induced beatings from her husband, although to call them beatings is to make an understatement of the highest order. They were not so much beatings as they were experiments designed to ascertain the many cumbersome ways to almost kill a sweet and gentle woman made of nothing but softness and.... Every thrashing, every night, became a journey into the deepest caverns of the souls of every slum dweller in sight. Her petrified pleas for forgiveness and mercy and her desperate confessions of transgressions, real and imagined, became our nightly prayers to the God we did not know but sought to appease, just in case He was real. There was no appeasing this beast of a man who only stopped when he had pummelled her unconscious. *There!* he would proclaim. *I have killed the witch!* Then he would stagger off into the eerily silent darkness that came just before the dawn. She never talked about her nightly torture but smiled and carried it like a gift box of secret precious things to her little shop made of corrugated iron sheets. Lulu neither rejoiced nor mourned when he was stabbed in what was, by all reports, a very ugly altercation at his favourite shebeen and left to bleed to death in a nearby ditch. She had simply buried the beast, gathered her children and walked back to her shop, her little place of solace. *Can you paint?* she asked me one day. *I want you write something for me.* She handed me a paintbrush with viscous globs of paint slowly dripping off the tip and began to dictate a moniker for her shop. That was the day her secret precious things were revealed for all to see in bright crimson calligraphy, '*Wathint' umfazi, wathint' imbokodo*'. You strike a woman you strike a rock.

This rock of a woman, who has smiled and offered me credit on her delicious warm *vetkoeks* that have sustained me and saved me from the grip of hunger, will not smile at me today. Today she will not see in me a faithful customer without whose patronage her business would have been a little worse off during these hard times. Her own suffering and torture forgotten, Lulu will become an enabler and the catalyst of the worst day of my life. She will not use the position of respect and favour she holds amongst the rabid pack that bays for my blood to plead my case for mercy. Oh no. She will choose rather to swing her motherly arms out to throw paraffin on the back of my shirt. As the warm slipperiness clings to my skin and I inhale noxious vapours I will ask myself, "*What have I done?*"

Behind me to the right Philip J., the septuagenarian *maître d'* from Malawi, will scream in his mother tongue and I will feel the terror in his voice reverberating through every cell in my body. Deaf from childhood he will not know why he is running for his life, as he cannot see the faces of his assailants in order to read their lips as they hurl abuse at him. The thing with Philip J.

though, is that he feels. Everything. He will have felt the savagery coming his way long before the attack. He will let out a spine chilling cry in anticipation of the man coming behind him who, thrusting a burning car tyre onto his shoulders and engulfing his head in flames and a thick column of black smoke, will end the old man's life in asphyxiation and terror. And probably more than just a little resignation and surrender. He's had a long run, overcome many an obstacle in post-colonial southern Africa, trekked from the foothills of Mount Mulanje in Malawi to this gold reef and worked a good long stint at the hands of some mean men and women who sought to subject him to all sorts of indignity, but he endeared himself to nearly all of them in the end. He's forgiven and forgotten and, at his age, he really doesn't need or want to fight this.

In the split second during which I pause, stunned by the horror that has befallen Philip, the horde that has gathered will fall upon me with sticks and boots and more of that toxic liquid gold will splatter all over me. Then, in a moment of completely irrational delirium, my mind will take me back to a clear-as-day memory of spending a night in a two-kilometre long queue of cars at a petrol station in Bulawayo, home.... Car owners lined up for petrol while the indigent queued for paraffin to light their primus stoves, desperately hoping to get some of the elusive petroleum product that now clings to my shirt and floods my lungs with death. How fitting that I should be born in Bulawayo, 'place of slaughter'. Bulawayo, my home town, place of strife and ethnic violence was founded by a group of Zulus fleeing King Shaka. I feel I have carried foreignness with me all along, my otherness is genetic and historic and predestined. All along this day has been coming. My fugitive forefathers deemed it so. My legs, burning with lactic acid and unable to sprint any longer, will collapse beneath me. These legs that carried me across the murky Limpopo and ran all night through South African fruit farms with the police, farmers and thugs hot on my heels, these legs that have walked the dingy streets of Johannesburg in search of a dream will decide that they owe me nothing more. When I fall to the ground I will turn to look up to heaven hoping to retreat to that formless, though comforting place, that I have built up in my mind, but instead I will see you light a match. Hateful coward that you will have become, you will pass the match to beautiful Masechaba, the stunning widow of an uMkhonto we Sizwe hero. How surreal it will be to gaze at her ageless face, this woman whose hips are the pride of Africa, and to watch her wrinkle her nose at me, spit into my stinging eyes and let the match drop with a slight upward curling of the corner of her mouth. As the little flame floats down towards me I will know that today is the day that I die. Today, alone, an outsider far from home, I will die because of what I am: an easy scapegoat on which your deep rooted sense of inadequacy can blame the continued failure of the black community to experience true freedom....

How strange it will feel to be aflame, to scramble again to my feet and to hear my own voice emerge from deep within my bowels. Every shack in this cesspool of poverty and silent suffering will hear the guttural, primal expression of a need so deep it defines both the hunter and the hunted, the need to be heard, the need to survive, the need to be saved...

I don't want to die. However, my flight will only serve to feed the flames and soon this man on fire will fall yet again and hope against all hope for some sort of redemption. But you will prove relentless and, armed with a burning rubber tyre, you will show me horror I would never have thought possible and hatred I have never known. I will smell for the first time in my life the tang of burning keratin as my hair is singed to nothing. I will become excruciatingly and intimately aware of each part of my body and how it responds to the pain and process of human combustion. Lungs already burning from the inside out sigh and collapse, eyes decide that they have seen enough and roll back leaving blood shot corneas which do not see puckering skin that was already black – too black some might say – pull away and recoil from itself. Arms and legs will flail wildly as misfiring neurones and scrambled messages cause suffocating muscles to spasm. Go. Stop. Go. Stop. Go. Go. Why won't you go?

This is the ugly part, where the adrenalin has worn off, your rage has subsided and the collective brain that told you that foreign is bad, that foreign steals jobs, that your brother is your enemy and that 'they' all deserve to die because your suffering is yours alone, will have no idea why it thought that in the first place. This is the part where the air hangs densely with shame, horror and silence and the mob has dissipated from fear of retribution. Retribution? From where? Remember, I am an outsider far away from home who will be described by a superficial yuppie news reporter as an *unidentified, alleged illegal immigrant in the Johannesburg slum of Dieplsloot, who was set ablaze by unknown attackers in what police are reluctant to call a xenophobic attack just forty days and forty nights after South Africa opened its doors to the world for the 2010 Football World Cup....*

The only person who will give me even a modicum of thought is the young ambitious journalist as he seeks to make his bones and edge his way towards becoming a famous news anchor, the face of 24 hour news. You will know this chap. You will very much like him, and trust him. He is a pretty boy, suave, clean shaven and has a winning smile that unfortunately fails to quite light up his eyes that secretly hunger for approval, recognition and fame. Already he sees himself among the ranks of Christiane Amanpour covering Bosnia or Bernard Shaw in the Gulf War, forgetting that these same heroes of the industry neglected to mention, in more than passing comment, the horrors of Rwanda. He sees himself changing the world and thinks he makes a difference, which perhaps he does, but maybe not so much for the benefit of me, the victim. Not today, anyway. He will not be the champion of my cause. I will not see retribution. There will be no consequences for what you will have done if you choose to do this to me.

As you set out to do me harm, consider, if you will, how it will feel to hunt me down and kill me. Consider the feeling when I am dead. Surely you will feel something? Will you ask yourself, *what have I done?* Perhaps not. For you will no longer be you, my friend, but a simple primate fighting for survival, all reason cast aside. Will you realise that you are nothing but a puppet whose strings are pulled by an unknown puppeteer? Will it occur to you that ever since he set eyes on you, this Geppetto has fed you lies, hollow stories and defeatist ideas about how there isn't enough. Not enough food to fill your stomach or enough books to feed your mind, not enough work to give you purpose and not enough room for you at the top. And you've repeated these lies to your children and your children's children so that by now, like Pinocchio, your communal nose is so long that it occludes a truth that once was so clear it needed no mention: *I am your brother.* Will you realise then that something is amiss in your rainbow nation and that someone has stolen the pot of gold, somebody else, not me?

My brother, hear me well. I do not want to die. Lying out in the open as my organs shut down like the lights of a many roomed house going off one by one, what remains is an unidentifiable hope born out of the greatest instinct of them all, survival. If we do indeed find ourselves having lived out this scenario to the moment where you have chosen to kill me because you have no other way of expressing your sense of disenfranchisement, then my sole remaining weapon will be my will to live. For one such as myself, an insatiable optimist for whom the future, unknown as it may be, is something to live for, filled with the promise of something to do and someone to love and worlds beyond worlds, life is an imperative that is hard to extinguish. I cannot let go. And so the battle comes down to my one last warrior, the one they call sentimental, the one accused of being deceitful but that supposedly

145

breaks at the hands of cruel lovers, the one they say is lacking in people who do evil and think nothing of it, that is said to bleed when confronted with the intolerable suffering of others, that burns when you eat too much, races when you are excited and aches when a loved one dies... a muscle the size of a fist. All I need is a beat. I will. Not die. I will. Not die. I will. Not die. I will. Not die.

A door slams shut. *Well?* You are looking at me quizzically. *You haven't heard a word I've said to you, have you?* What? My heart is racing. Sunlight burns my eyes and I realise we have disembarked from the minibus and I am standing sweaty-palmed and breathless on the side of the road. *You didn't even get her number, did you, m'fethu?* you ask rhetorically, shaking your head as you saunter to the corner to buy yourself some *vetkoeks* while all around me people are rushing off to get ahead on another bright and crispy winter's day.

Glossary

amadlozi – ancestral spirits

aiwa – no

born-free – slang for a Zimbabwean born after the country's independence in 1980

born-location – urban slang for children born and raised in urban areas

braai – barbecue

chigamba – patch of fabric used to mend a tear in a garment

chimurenga – the Zimbabwean liberation struggle, specifically that of the 1970s

dare – court

doek – head scarf

gonyet – truck

hokoyo – look out

hure – whore

isitshwala – thick maize-meal porridge

jete – dominant woman

khaya – home

knobkerrie – short wooden club

kombi – urban public transportation, usually a minibus

kwerekwere – derogatory term referring to a foreigner of African origin

kugara nhaka – the handing over of a widowed woman to one of her deceased husband's male relatives as a wife

kumusha – rural folk

laat lammetjie – afterthought

lomuntu uyasinyatsa – this person is disrespecting us

mabhanzi – buns

mabhunu – pejorative term for white farmers

mafutha – fatty

mahewu – unfermented beer

maiguru – big mother (elder wife)

mainini – small mother (younger wife)

mandebvu – he of the long beard

manyathela – sandals made out of pieces of old tyres

mapostori – African Apostolic church groups

mari – money

masese – sour opaque beer

mbodza – runny sadza that has failed to thicken and set due to poor cookery

mudhara – old man

mhandara – virgin

mhoro – hello

m'fethu – colloquial term meaning brother

mtengesi – sellout

muchakasara moma Chivi – in the deep remote parts of Chivi

muribho – are you well?

murungu – white person

muti – medicine

mwanangu – my child

mzungu – white person

netara – by tarred road

ngonjo – policeman

nyanga – medicine man

pata-patas – flip flops

piri-piri – hot pepper

pondok – crudely made house built of tin sheets, reeds, etc

robots – traffic lights

roora – bride price

sadza – thick maize-meal porridge

saka rini – when

sungura – type of music

tina haikona choncha – we are not stealing

tokoloshe – dwarf-like mischievous and evil spirit

tsotsi – thief

umnumzana – rough equivalent of gentleman

vanababa – fathers

varoyi – witches

varumwe – men

vasahwira – friend

vasikana – ladies

vatate – aunt

vauya – they have come

vetkoeks – traditional Afrikaner pastry, made from frying dough

wengu – mine

yowee kani – oh my gosh (a lament)

Contributors

Raisedon Baya is an award winning playwright, director, author and arts administrator resident in Bulawayo. Some of his best plays can be found in his anthology *Tomorrow's People*. Raisedon also writes a regular arts column for a weekly national paper and has had short stories published in magazines and several anthologies.

NoViolet Bulawayo is a writer and aspiring filmmaker. She recently earned her MFA at Cornell University, where her work has been recognized with a Truman Capote Fellowship. She teaches creative writing and composition at Cornell and is "putting the absolute final touches to a novel." A version of *Snapshots* was a finalist for the 2009 SA Pen/Studzinski Award and her short story *Hitting Budapest* won the 2011 Caine Prize for African Writing.

Diana Charsley is a Zimbabwean who has had several short stories published in anthologies. She's keen on God and works for the Bulawayo Help Network.

Mapfumo Clement Chihota recently migrated to New Zealand, where he lives with his family. Previously, he studied and taught at the University of Cape Town and, prior to that, worked at the Zimbabwe Open University. Clement has had poems published in Zimbabwe and South Africa, and short stories in Zimbabwe, South Africa, the USA and the UK.

Murenga Joseph Chikowero is a graduate student at the University of Wisconsin-Madison. He has had short stories published online with *StoryTime*.

John Eppel's first novel, *D G G Berry's The Great North Road*, won the M-Net prize and his second, *Hatchings*, was short-listed for the M-Net prize and was chosen for the series in the *Times Literary Supplement* of the most significant books to have come out of Africa. His other novels are *The Giraffe Man*, *The Curse of the Ripe Tomato*, *The Holy Innocents* and *Absent: The English Teacher*.
His poetry collections include *Spoils of War*, which won the Ingrid Jonker Prize, *Sonata for Matabeleland*, *Selected Poems: 1965- 1995* and *Songs My*

Country Taught Me. He has written two collections of poetry and short stories: *The Caruso of Colleen Bawn* and *White Man Crawling*.
A collection of stories and poems, *Together*, by John and the late Julius Chingono was published in 2011.

Fungai Rufaro Machirori is a poet, trained journalist, blogger, researcher and short story writer. She has worked in HIV and AIDS communication, research and documentation in Zimbabwe and South Africa, and was honoured in 2007 with an Africa-wide award for excellence in strategic HIV and AIDS communication. Last year, she was published in an anthology of Zimbabwean women's poetry entitled *Sunflowers in You Eyes*. She is currently studying towards a Masters Degree in Development Studies in the United Kingdom.

Barbara Mhangami-Ruwende was born and raised in Zimbabwe. She left home at the age of eighteen and worked in Germany before embarking on her undergraduate studies at the University of Glasgow. Barbara moved to the United States in 1997, where she resides with her husband and four daughters. She is passionate about raising her daughters, reading good literature, writing and running marathons.

Christopher Mlalazi has had short stories published in anthologies in Zimbabwe, South Africa and the United Kingdom, as well as on the web. In 2008, Christopher won the Oxfam Novib PEN Freedom of ExpressionAward. His first collection of short stories, *Dancing with Life: Tales from the Township*, won a 2009 Zimbabwe National Arts Merit Award and was awarded an Honourable Mention at the 2009 Noma Awards for African Publishing. His first novel, *Many Rivers*, was published in 2009. Christopher was a 2010 Feuchtwanger Fellow and a 2011 Nordic Africa Institute Guest Writer. *They Are Coming* is an adaptation of the first chapter of his as yet unpublished novel *Autumn Leaves*.

Mzana Mthimkhulu was born at Mpilo Hospital, just across the street from Barbourfields stadium, home to Highlanders Football Club. At twenty, he conceded that his desire to play for Highlanders Under 19s was unrealistic and he turned his attention to the first team. Not having made it to the reserve side by the time he was thirty, he set his sights on the position of Head Coach. At forty, he almost made it to the position of sidekick to assistant coach.

Never one to give up easily, he is currently gunning to chair the club. Whilst waiting for this inevitable appointment, Mzana kills time writing fiction and social commentaries and being a human resources practitioner. Married with three children, Mzana loves the fragrance of old books and the sight of a hen with its chicks.

Blessing Musariri is a published and award-winning children's author who writes many other things besides. Her publications to date are *Rufaro's Day, Going Home: A Tree's Story* and *The Mystery of Rokodzi Mountain*. She has short stories and poems published in various international anthologies and online magazines. Blessing mistakenly believed she would be a lawyer but her prolific and overactive imagination took over, after sitting and passing the English Bar Finals in 1997, and led her to a more varied, unpredictable but immensely fulfilling life in the world of arts and culture. She also holds a Masters in Diplomatic Studies (with distinction) from the University of Westminster. Blessing mostly lives in Harare, but is very often to be found up in the air, going some place else.

Nyevero Muza, married with two children, is a banker by profession. He runs a financial advisory firm he co-founded in Harare and doubles as a financial columnist with a local daily newspaper. Nyevero holds a banking diploma and an MBA. He has had several stories published online. As well as writing in his spare time he plays guitar.

Thabisani Ndlovu was born in Lupane in 1971 and completed his schooling in Bulawayo. He has recently been awarded a PhD from the University of the Witwatersrand. Thabisani has published short stories in several anthologies, including *Creatures Great and Small, Short Writings from Bulawayo III, Long Time Coming: Short Writings from Zimbabwe* and *The Caine Prize for African Writing, 2009.*

Bryony Rheam was born in Kadoma in 1974 and lived in Bulawayo from the age of eight until she left school. She studied for a BA and an MA in English Literature in the United Kingdom and then taught in Singapore for a year before returning to teach in Zimbabwe from 2001 to 2008. Still a teacher, she now lives in Ndola, Zambia. Bryony has had short stories in many Zimbabwe anthologies and her first novel, *This September Sun*, won Best First Book at the 2010 Zimbabwe Book Publishers Association Awards.

Novuyo Rosa Tshuma has had short fiction published in several anthologies including *The Bed Book of Short Stories* and *A Life In Full and Other Stories: Caine Prize Anthology 2010*. She was the winner of the Intwasa Short Story Competition 2009. Currently, she is pursuing her studies at the University of Witwatersrand, South Africa. She has attended workshops such as the Farafina Summer Writing Workshop 2010 and the Caine Prize Africa Writing Workshop 2010 in Kenya.

Sandisile Tshuma, having been born and raised in Bulawayo, returned to the city after three years studying Chemical, Molecular and Cellular Sciences at the University of Cape Town, to study Development and Disaster Management at the National University of Science and Technology. At present she lives in Johannesburg and works as Programme Associate for the UNESCO East and Southern Africa EDUCAIDS programme. Sandisile's short story, *Arrested Development*, from *Long Time Coming: Short Writings from Zimbabwe*, was awarded an Honourable Mention in the 2010 Thomas Pringle Awards for the best short story published in a newspaper or journal in southern Africa in the preceding two years.

other 'amaBooks titles
include

Together
by Julius Chingono and John Eppel

This September Sun
by Bryony Rheam

Long Time Coming: Short Writings from Zimbabwe
edited by Jane Morris

Dancing with Life: Tales from the Township
by Christopher Mlalazi

Intwasa Poetry
edited by Jane Morris